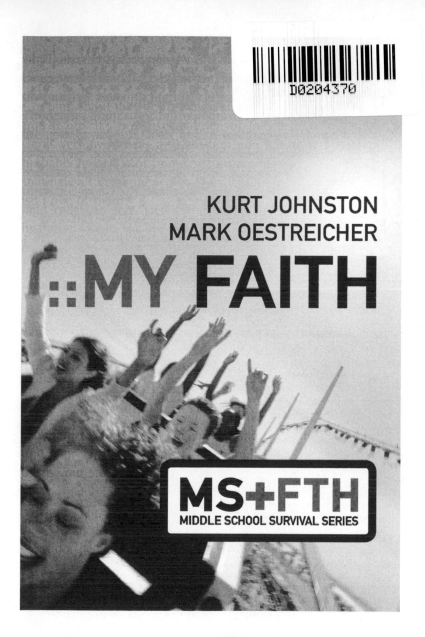

KURT JOHNSTON
MARK OESTREICHER

[::MY FAITH

MS+FTH
MIDDLE SCHOOL SURVIVAL SERIES

ZONDERVAN®

invert
www.invertbooks.com

ZONDERVAN.com/
AUTHORTRACKER
follow your favorite authors

My Faith: Middle School Survival Series
Copyright © 2007 by Kurt Johnston & Mark Oestreicher

Youth Specialties products, 300 S. Pierce St., El Cajon, CA 92020 are published by Zondervan, 5300 Patterson Ave. SE, Grand Rapids, MI 49530.

Library of Congress Cataloging-in-Publication Data

Oestreicher, Mark.
  My faith / by Mark Oestreicher and Kurt Johnston.
      p. cm. — (Middle school survival series)
  Includes bibliographical references and index.
  ISBN-10: 0-310-27382-X (pbk. : alk. paper)
  ISBN-13: 978-0-310-27382-0 (pbk. : alk. paper)
  1. Christian life—Juvenile literature. 2. Middle school students—Religious life—Juvenile literature. I. Johnston, Kurt, 1966- II. Title.
  BV4531.3.O38 2006
  248.8'3—dc22

                                                                  2006024014

This edition printed on acid-free paper.

Creative Team: Dave Urbanski, Erika Hueneke, Janie Wilkerson, Rich Cairnes, and Mark Novelli
Cover Design by Gearbox

Printed in the United States of America

---

10 11 12 • 23 22 21 20 19 18 17 16 15 14 13 12 11 10 9 8

DEDICATION

This book is dedicated to our two favorite middle school girls in the entire universe: Kayla Rae Johnston and Liesl Maria Oestreicher. These girls—our girls—are their daddies' pride and joy. And both of them really want to live like Jesus, so we're pretty pumped about that, too!

ACKNOWLEDGMENTS

Marko wants to thank his amazing family—Jeannie, Liesl, and Max—for being so loving, and for your patience while I was writing this. I also want to thank the great peeps of YS, for letting me be an author while we continue to work together. I need to thank my friend Brian McLaren for the use of six of his seven "C-words" to describe God's Big Story (from his book, *The Story We Find Ourselves In*) and a couple of illustrations. And thanks to the fine people of the Starbucks at Chase and Avocado in El Cajon, for a great writing spot, wi-fi access, and a good stream of strong coffee.

Kurt wants to thank Rachel, Kayla, and Cole—my incredible family—for giving up some time with me so I could work on this book. Thank you to my partners in junior high ministry at Saddleback Church. It's because of your incredible giftedness, passion, and dedication to our ministry that I find myself with a little extra time to write. I also want to thank my junior highers—I enjoy writing, but I *love* being your pastor. And yes, the people at Starbucks in Rancho Santa Margarita...I'm a wimp, so I don't drink coffee, but you make a delicious vanilla steamer that warms my stomach while I write.

CONTENTS

INTRODUCTION   8

SECTION 1: LET'S START AT THE BEGINNING   11

Who Is God?   12

God's Original Plan   14

The Sin Club   16

Reconciliation: Not So Silly   18

God's Big Story in Seven Mini-Chapters, Part 1 (Creation)   20

God's Big Story in Seven Mini-Chapters, Part 2 (Crisis)   22

God's Big Story in Seven Mini-Chapters, Part 3 (Calling)   24

God's Big Story in Seven Mini-Chapters, Part 4 (Conversation)   26

God's Big Story in Seven Mini-Chapters, Part 5 (Christ)   28

God's Big Story in Seven Mini-Chapters, Part 6 (Community)   30

God's Big Story in Seven Mini-Chapters, Part 7 (Commencement)   32

SECTION 2: FAITH AND DOUBT   37

What Is Faith?   38

How Do I Get More Faith?   40

Moses' Mom and Freak-Faith   42

Doubts: Why They're Normal   44

Doubts: What to Do about Them   46

Doubts: How Jesus Handled Them   48

Child*like* Faith and Child*ish* Faith   50

Upgrading Your Operating System   52

Learn from Demas (about Chucking Your Faith)   54

What If I Don't Feel Like a Christian?   56

SECTION 3: BIBLE STUFF   59

Where Did the Bible Come From?   60

How Can I Be Sure the Bible Is True?   62

The Role of the Bible   64

Cool Ways to Use the Bible (besides Just Reading It)   66

Bible Sayings I've Heard but May Not Totally Understand: *Salt* and *Light*   68

Bible Sayings I've Heard but May Not Totally Understand: *Vine and Branches*   70

Bible Sayings I've Heard but May Not Totally Understand: *The Good Shepherd*   72

A Few Bible Verses Worth Remembering   74

SECTION 4: PRAYER   79

How to Pray   80

Other Ways to Pray   82

SECTION 5: THE CHURCH AND WORSHIP   85

What Is the Church?   86

Do I Have to Go to Church to Be a Christian?   88

What Do These Words Mean?   90

What Is Worship?   92

SECTION 6: COMMON QUESTIONS ABOUT CHRISTIANITY   95

Aren't All Religions Basically the Same?   96

What's the Trinity All About?   98

How Can God Be Everywhere and Know Everything?   100

If God Is So Good, Why Is There So Much Bad Stuff?   102

SECTION 7: SPIRITUAL GROWTH   105

How Can I Grow in My Faith?   106

Where Can I Find God?   108

Playing It Safe = A Stupid, Boring Life   110

How to Be the Coolest Transformer   112

How's Your Reflection? (Reflecting Jesus)   114

How to Bounce Back When I've Messed Up   116

What Difference Do My Friends Make?   118

SECTION 8: A FEW BIBLE PEEPS   123

Jael and Tough Stuff   124

Samson and Spiritual Priorities   126

Peter and Steppin' Out   128

How Much Does God Love Me? (Hosea and Gomer)   130

God Loves Losers (Mighty Men in 1 and 2 Samuel) 132

Eleazar and Standing Alone 134

Aaron and Hur and the Importance of Christian Friends 136

SECTION 9: WHAT'S GOD WANT OUTTA ME? 139

What Does God Want Outta Me? 140

Why Does God Care If I Grow? 142

The Big List O' Rules (Really Just Two!) 144

Does God Really Have a Plan for My Life? 146

How to Live for Jesus without Looking Like a Jerk 148

My Part in God's Family 150

How to Share My Story with My Friends 152

Giving My Time 154

Giving My Talents 156

Giving My Money and My Stuff 158

Nobody Said It Would Be Easy 160

SECTION 10: SOME OF THE BIGGIES YOU'LL FACE 163

Peer Pressure 164

Temptation 166

Making Wise Choices 168

SECTION 11: RANDOM SURVIVAL TIPS 173

God Sings about You! 174

What's an Heir? 176

How to Figure Out How You're Wired 178

SECTION 12: WISDOM RULES 181

Wisdom Rule #1—Be Like an Ant! 182

Wisdom Rule #2—Be Like a Coney! 184

Wisdom Rule #3—Be Like a Locust! 186

Wisdom Rule #4—Be Like a Lizard! 188

INTRODUCTION

See this first really dorky photo? That's me, Marko, in middle school. Nice shirt collar, huh? Can you tell just by looking at my picture that I wasn't the most popular kid in school? Uh, yeah.

How about this second groovy shot? That's me, Kurt, in middle school. That haircut rocked, huh? Sure, whatever.

We wanted you to see those pictures—as embarrassing as they are—because we want you to know that we remember what it's like to be a middle school student. Partly, we remember because both of us have been working with middle schoolers in churches for a long time. We don't work with high school kids or with any other age group. That's because both of us are convinced of a few things:

- First, that middle schoolers are the coolest people in the world. Really, we'd rather hang out with a group of middle school students than any other age group.

- Next, that God really cares (we mean, really cares) about middle school students—about you. And we're convinced that God is stoked about the possibility of having a close relationship with you.

- Finally, that the middle school years (about 11 to 14) are hugely important in building a faith that will last for your whole life.

What you're holding in your hands is the first book in the brand-new Middle School Survival Series. This first book is all about your faith (duh, that's what the title says!). And the second book is about your family. We have more books planned in the series on friends, changes, future, and school. We hope you'll read them all!

Oh, one more thing: You don't have to read these 75 "chapters" in any particular order. It's not that kind of book. You can read them in order if you want (if you're one of those people who likes order), or you can flip through and read whatever catches your attention.

We really believe in you, and we'll be praying for you (really, we will) that while you read this, you'll grow in your understanding (just like the Bible says Jesus did when he was your age) of God and how much he loves you—how he would do anything to let you know him!

Kurt and Marko

LET'S START AT THE BEGINNING

WHO IS GOD?

BIBLE FACT: THE LAST WORD IN THE BIBLE IS *AMEN* (REVELATION 22:21).

You're probably holding this book in your hands because you already believe in God; most people do. But even though most people believe in God, there's a good chance they don't really know *who he is.*

All through history, people have worshiped all sorts of gods. Many times they would create gods that fit what was happening in their lives. They might have had a god of the hunt to help out when they went hunting or a god of battle to help them when they fought a war. Not a bad idea...I could have used a "god of the kiss" to help out when I kissed a girl for the first time, but that's an entirely different story.

Although a custom-made god for various situations may seem pretty cool, it's not the way it is. The Bible makes it clear that there is one true God. Yep, one God who spoke the heavens into existence, created people out of dirt, and holds the world in his hand.

In the Bible, God says he is the "First and the Last...the Beginning and the End" (Revelation 22:13). In other words, God has always been and will always be...there is no beginning or end to God because, well, because he *is* the beginning and the end! Wow, think about that for a second...but not too long, or else your brain will start to hurt.

Here are a few other cool things about God: God knows everything, is everywhere at one time, is all-powerful, and is the source of all creation. But here's the best part: God wants a relationship with you and has a plan for your life! Imagine that...the all-knowing, all-powerful, everywhere-at-once God knows you and hopes you'll want to know him.

How do you get to know God? By reading the Bible, by getting to know Jesus (Jesus is God in human form...God in a bod!), by talking to God in prayer, and stuff like that.

It takes faith to believe in the one true God. It isn't always a popular route to take. But even though we'll never know and understand everything about him, we can know that he's ready, willing, and able to be a part of our lives!

GOD'S ORIGINAL PLAN

How many times have you heard your parents, teachers, coaches, or youth pastor ask, "What were you thinking?"

We've worked with middle school students for a long time, and both of us have middle school children. If we had a nickel for every time we've asked young teenagers that question, we'd have enough money to open our own Starbucks (which happens to be where much of this book was written).

It seems as though every time we've asked that question, we've been given the same answer: "I dunno." Sometimes you just kinda do what you feel like, and sometimes it makes sense to those around you...and sometimes it doesn't. It isn't just you; we all do it. Most people don't usually take the time to think through their actions. Instead they act first, and then, based on how things turn out, they decide if it was the right choice.

It's easy to look at the world we live in and wonder, *God, what were you thinking?* Believe it or not, God did have an original plan in mind when he created us. Since God knows everything, it would be kinda freaky if he answered that question with, "I dunno"!

So, just what was his plan? Are you ready? Drumroll, please (insert your own drumroll sound here): The Bible says that we were made *by* God and *for* God. His original plan for all humans was for us to have a perfect, joy-filled relationship with him. That should make you feel pretty good. If you take the time to read the first couple of chapters in Genesis, you'll see that God created Adam and Eve and placed them in the Garden of Eden. The Garden of Eden was a beautiful, lush land filled with everything they needed, including God's presence. In the garden, Adam and Eve had a very special friendship with God.

> "SOMETIMES IT'S HARD FOR ME TO BELIEVE THAT GOD ACTUALLY WANTS TO BE MY FRIEND."
>
> —MELANIE, SEVENTH GRADE

So what was God thinking? What was his original plan? To provide a place for people to live in comfort, protection, and perfect relationship with him so he could enjoy us, his incredible creation!

THE SIN CLUB

Have you ever done, thought, or said anything wrong? Have you ever decided not to do the right thing? Welcome to the club...a very big club! It's the Sin Club. Sin includes stuff like stealing and cheating, but there's more to it than that.

One way to define sin is, "To miss the mark." In olden days when somebody shot an arrow at a target and missed the bull's-eye, the judge would yell, "Sin," which signaled to everyone that the shooter missed the mark...the perfect bull's-eye. In the Bible, God gives us a whole bunch of marks, or bull's-eyes, to aim for, and because God is perfect, his bull's-eye can be pretty tough for people to hit. God has a pretty high standard for how he hopes we will treat others, how we will make choices, and how we will handle life. When we miss the mark, we have sinned. Instead of listing a whole bunch of sins and creating some sort of checklist, let's take a look at two big categories that just about every sin falls into:

Sins of commission: This is a fancy term that simply means there are sins that are a direct result of stuff we choose to do or stuff we choose to think. Choosing to cheat or steal would be sins of commission.

Sins of omission: This is another fancy term that means there are sins that are a result of stuff we know we *should* do but choose not to do, like when your friend has hurt your feelings and you refuse to forgive her, or when your dad asks you to take out the trash and you don't. In both cases, your choice *not* to do something was a sin.

It's important to remember that a mistake isn't a sin. When you accidentally track mud on your mom's carpet or knock over your dad's golf clubs in the garage, you haven't sinned. You've just made an honest mistake.

It's also important not to let yourself become the "sin police," pointing out all the sins your family and friends are guilty of. The religious leaders in the Bible loved to do this...they thought they were better than everybody else and loved to point out the sins people were guilty of. The funny thing is that the religious leaders were actually worse because they should have known better. Even though they looked good on the outside, they had all kinds of gross stuff going on in their hearts.

Sin always begins in the heart, so protect your heart!

RECONCILIATION: NOT SO SILLY

Reconciliation...that's a biggie! Every now and then in this book we're going to drop some big words on you—words you can use to thrill and amaze your friends.

Let's review a little bit and set the stage: Earlier we talked about God's original plan—to have a perfect, joy-filled relationship with us. Next we talked a little bit about sin...when we miss God's mark. What we didn't cover is the fact that sin is what messed up God's original plan. Remember when we said that the Sin Club is a really big club? That's because Adam and Eve were the first to sin, and everybody since then has joined their club...every single one of us has sinned.

Adam and Eve were enjoying a perfect, joy-filled relationship with God until they messed things up by disobeying him and eating from the forbidden tree. They didn't mess things up just for them, but for you, too, because that first sin paved the way for all the sin that has followed. But hey, don't go pointing your fingers at Adam and Eve (remember, don't be the sin police!)—you would have done the same thing. Sin hurt their relationships with God, and sin hurts our relationships with God, too.

But God's original plan is still the same...he wants a relationship with us, and in order for this to happen, we need *reconciliation*.

Reconciliation really just means "restoring a relationship," or getting a relationship back to where it's supposed to be. Sin messed up humans' relationship with God, and he wants to restore it.

> "IT SEEMS LIKE I MESS UP ALL THE TIME.
> I'M GLAD JESUS DOESN'T GET TIRED OF FORGIVING ME!"
>
> —MICAH, EIGHTH GRADE

So, why doesn't God just forgive us and move on? He does! Through Jesus, the only person to never sin, God became a human being and allowed himself to pay for our sins so that we could have reconciliation with God...so our relationship with God could be restored to the way he originally wanted it to be.

Even though none of us will ever be perfect (although Marko's pretty dang close), we can have a relationship with God because Jesus allowed himself to die and then came back to life!

GOD'S BIG STORY IN SEVEN MINI-CHAPTERS, PART 1 (CREATION)

It wasn't *that* long ago that you started reading chapter books, was it? And you know how different they are from the books you read as a little kid. Chapter books break the story into different parts rather than just telling a single scene. But chapter books still tell one story—just with a *ton* more detail.

So it is with God's story, told to us through the Bible. There are 66 books, but they're all part of telling one *big* story. Because many of the Bible books tell the same parts of God's Big Story, just from different "camera angles," we're going to make it a bit simpler for you. We're going to summarize God's Big Story in seven mini-chapters—from before the beginning to after the end! (And to make it easier to remember, we're going to use seven words that start with the letter *C*.)

Chapter 1, most of you could guess, is...*Creation.*

God chose to invent something totally outside of himself. And—this is so important—God chose to create something that would re-create itself. You can *start* to understand this by thinking of *The Sims*, or some other simulation game where you choose parts and the parts "decide" what to do next. But that's not a perfect way to think about it because those simulation games are still programmed by humans. God chose to invent a world where things (like you and me) really *do* have a choice. What a wild idea!

And then God does this totally cool thing: He invites us to play a role in this amazing creation—to be co-creators *with* him! You create stuff every day, and not just when you build something or draw something. You create something by how you live, by how you treat people, by every choice you make. Your presence on this earth changes things! We can change things for good or change things for bad—but we *do* change things, even when we're not thinking about it.

That's the amazing first mini-chapter of God's Big Story: God *created* a world that keeps on re-creating, and he invites us to join in the process!

GOD'S BIG STORY IN SEVEN MINI-CHAPTERS, PART 2 (CRISIS)

In the first mini-chapter, God *created* everything out of nothing. Whoa!

But mini-chapter 2, unfortunately, is next—*Crisis*.

(When you read "crisis," you need to make a little "beep-beep-beep" warning sound like when, in a movie, the really cute girl tells the guy who likes her, "I'm actually a zombie, and I've come here to eat your stomach.") Into God's perfect creation comes the nasty, evil villain of *crisis*. And guess who brings it? No, not that mean kid from your fourth-period math class. It's *you* and *me*! *We* are the ones who bring *crisis* into God's perfect *creation*.

Well, to be fair, let's back up a bit (did you back up?). I mean, let's back up a few years. Adam and Eve—heard of 'em? First peeps—ring a bell? They were chillin' in a totally perfect world (the Bible calls it "Eden," or "the Garden of Eden"). But they weren't exactly happy about the few boundaries God put in place—boundaries that were put there to protect them.

Adam and Eve crossed the boundaries, and—BAM!—hello, *crisis*.

Time-travel forward just a bit. Heard of "the Tower of Babel"? It was in this city (called Babel) where the people decided they were smart enough to build a tower all the way to heaven. BAM! More *crisis*.

Here's the key: The people of Babel didn't think they needed God anymore.

That's the way most of us (yeah, you included) still bring crisis into God's perfect creation today. We decide we don't really need God (maybe not in everything—but in this thing, or that thing), and we cross the boundaries God put in place for our own protection. BAM! More *crisis!* Let's face it: We're *crisis*-bringers.

What's one part of your life (big part or little part) where you're living as if you don't need God, and you're crossing his boundaries?

GOD'S BIG STORY IN SEVEN MINI-CHAPTERS, PART 3 (CALLING)

What a mess! Everything was perfect and peachy after mini-chapter 1, *Creation*. But then stupid mini-chapter 2 had to show up, thanks to us! We brought *crisis* into God's perfect *creation*, messing it all up. Silly people!

But don't panic! Mini-chapter 3 is a pretty amazing fixer. It starts with a dude named Abraham (let's call him Abe). I hope you've heard of Abe, because he's one of the most important people in the history of faith! Abe was a wild man, a revolutionary, and not because he had a nose-spike or a yellow Mohawk or something. Abe was a radical guy because he became convinced there was *only one God*. Now that might not sound all that radical to you—but *no one* believed that when Abe lived. Everyone (really, *everyone*—talk about peer pressure!) worshiped thousands of gods...or what they *thought* were gods.

But our Abe—he was *the man*! And he chose to believe in our God. The one true God. In response God turned the page to mini-chapter 3: *Calling*.

You can read it for yourself in Genesis 12:1-3, but God basically says, "Abe, I want you to leave everything and everyone you know, and I want you to go somewhere. I'm not going to tell you where you're going yet, but it's going to be really, really good. Oh, and Abe? The reason I'm doing this, the reason I'm blessing you like this, is because I want you to be a blessing to *everyone* else."

Here's the deal (this is super important): The *calling* chapter *starts* with Abe, but it continues on to you and me. God's call wasn't just a one-time deal. God is still *calling* us, to leave stuff behind and go where he tells us to go—knowing that it's going to be great for us. And, get this, God's *calling* is still the same: *I'm going to bless you so you can be a blessing to others.*

See? God's amazing plan for righting some of the *crisis* we bring into his perfect *creation* is to invite us (really, it's more "telling" than "inviting") to be a blessing to the world. That's our *calling*.

GOD'S BIG STORY IN SEVEN MINI-CHAPTERS, PART 4 (CONVERSATION)

Are you keeping up with the C-words that describe the chapters of God's Big Story? So far we have: *Creation, crisis,* and *calling.*

And we've only gotten through the first few chapters of Genesis—the very first book in the Bible! At this rate, we could have 4,379 chapters, or something like that. That wouldn't be very easy to remember!

But there's good news: The next chapter covers (this is huge, maybe we should have another drumroll) the rest of the entire Old Testament! That's right—three chapters of the story in half of a Bible book; then one more chapter in thirty-eight and a half more Bible books.

There's a reasonable explanation for this, we promise. And to explain it, you need to know that we're calling the fourth mini-chapter, *Conversation.*

There's a ton of great stuff in the rest of the Old Testament—stories that will rock your world and truths about God and our lives that you just gotta read. But in terms of God's Big Story, from the beginning of time all the way out past us into the future, the rest of the Old Testament can be summarized as a conversation between God and his people, the Jews.

And we have a really fun way to remember the order of the biggie Old Testament stories: *Up, middle, down, mmmiddle, up, middle.* Got that?

I know it'll make you feel really stupid, but it really helps to remember this if you stand up and then say the words while moving your body up and down. Oh, and when you say "mmmiddle" and stand back up, you have to swivel your hips like a hula dancer.

Here are the story connections. It's based on a map: Abe was *up* in a country in the North (of the Middle East, that is, where all the Bible stuff took place), and God *called* Abe to leave his home and go south to the *middle*. A while later, Joseph got sold into slavery by his brothers and was taken farther south (all the way to Egypt, in northern Africa), way *down*. A few generations passed, and God sent Moses to free the Hebrew people from Egypt and go back up to the Promised Land in the *mmmiddle* (okay, so the reason you have to do the hula thing and hold out that "m" is that the Hebrew people wandered around in the desert for a long time on their way to the middle). A buncha years later, enemy armies captured most of the Hebrew people and took them *up* to their own countries. But eventually some of them got to return back to the *middle* to rebuild their homes.

Whew! That could almost make you dizzy!

A last thought on this mini-chapter of *conversation*: Like all the other chapters, this one still continues. God continues his conversation with us today—or, at least, he *wants* to.

Are you willing to have a conversation with God?

GOD'S BIG STORY IN SEVEN MINI-CHAPTERS, PART 5 (CHRIST)

Oh, man, we're excited (Kurt and Marko, that is). I bet you can guess the next C-word! Remember, we just finished the entire Old Testament with the previous word: *Conversation*. So we're on to the New Testament...which means we're jumping into the books called "the Gospels" (Matthew, Mark, Luke, and John)...and those books tell the amazing and life-changing (really, world- and everything-changing!) story of Jesus...so, the next C-word, the fifth mini-chapter in God's Big Story, must be...*Christ*! Yeah, we knew you knew.

By the way, *Jesus* was (and is) a first name, just like ours are (Marko and Kurt). But *Christ* means "anointed one" and is the same as the word *Messiah*. People used to refer to Jesus as "Jesus *the* Christ," and somewhere along the line, we all just dropped the word *the*. In other words, *Christ* wasn't Jesus' last name!

Okay, this is important. Jesus didn't just start to exist at this point in God's Big Story. Jesus has been there all along. In fact, John 1:1-3 tells us that Jesus was actually the creator back in mini-chapter 1 (*Creation*).

But a wild and radical thing happens here in mini-chapter 5: Jesus (*Christ*) becomes human so he can invite us into God's Big Story. Jesus became his own invention (whoa, that will blow your mind if you think about it). And just like the other chapters where you're invited to join in, this chapter is all about joining in, too.

See, Jesus said and taught lots of things. But the summary of all of what he said, the main question he came to ask (and is still asking you today) is, "Will you follow me?" And that's because following Jesus is the very, very best way to live—not just for us, but also for the whole world.

So, do you? Do you want to follow Jesus?

When Jesus died on the cross, it seemed to many that his message of hope was just a nice idea that couldn't really work.

But when he came back to life three days later, he proved that God's story of grace and forgiveness is better than any other story.

GOD'S BIG STORY IN SEVEN MINI-CHAPTERS, PART 6 (COMMUNITY)

After Jesus' death and resurrection (after the *Christ* chapter), the church got rolling. But *church* isn't the C-word we're going to use for the next chapter. We're calling it *Community*.

But let's back up to *Christ* for a second. You're probably aware of the idea that Jesus is our *master*. But there are a couple of ways of using the word *master*. The first way is like "boss" and is really the language of slavery (a slave has a master). But there's another way to use *master*: It's used for someone who is the very, very best at something. The best violin players in the world are called "master violin players." You could even say the best Xbox player is a *master*. Let's think of Jesus this way: Yes, Jesus came to earth to bring a way for us to know God. But Jesus also came to show us how to live! Jesus is the master of living the best way, and he gives us a perfect example to follow.

So almost all the stuff in the New Testament, after the four Gospels that tell the *Christ* story, is about the *Community* of the master. It starts out as a group of people totally committed to following the ways of their master (Jesus) and continues on to you and us! Remember, this is our story, too! And this part of God's Big Story, connecting with our story and your story, is all about us learning (or trying to learn!) to follow our master.

How's that going for you? Are you committed to following Jesus' perfect example of how to live? Are you committed to being part of a *community* that's trying to live like our master, Jesus *Christ?*

GOD'S BIG STORY IN SEVEN MINI-CHAPTERS, PART 7 (COMMENCEMENT)

A quick review:

Mini-chapter 1—*Creation* (God makes everything out of nothing.)

Mini-chapter 2—*Crisis* (We cross God's boundaries and mess up his perfect *creation.*)

Mini-chapter 3—*Calling* (God calls Abraham, and us, to be a blessing to the world.)

Mini-chapter 4—*Conversation* (God begins a long conversation with his people—first the Hebrew people, but continuing on with us.)

Mini-chapter 5—*Christ* (Woo-hoo! Jesus comes and lives with us, giving us both a way to connect with God and the example of a master.)

Mini-chapter 6—*Community* (We're invited to be a part of a community that follows the master, Jesus.)

And finally the last chapter of God's Big Story: *Commencement.*

What's one of the best things about middle school? Graduating from it! Same is true in high school. And that ceremony they have when you officially wrap it up and move on is called *commencement.* Most of the time we think of that ceremony as the *end* of something. But it's really more about the *beginning* of something else. Even the word itself means that: To *commence* means to begin something (not to end something).

The last chapter in God's Big Story is about an end to the way things are now—and about the beginning of the most amazing life *after* the way things are now. Think of a couple of dog owners taking their pup to the park on a leash. They get to a big open field, and one owner goes to the other side of the field without the dog. Then the owner with the dog releases the dog from the leash, and the owner on the far side of the field calls the dog. Here's the trippy part: In this illustration, we're like the dog (sorry!), and God is *both* owners! God started everything with *creation*, and he *calls* to us from the future (that will make your brain hurt if you think about it!).

You want a description of heaven? It's the place where all God's dreams and hopes for his *creation* come true. And all of us who have chosen to make our stories part of God's Big Story get to be a part of that!

There you have it. God's Big Story in seven mini-chapters: *Creation, Crisis, Calling, Conversation, Christ, Community,* and *Commencement.* And if you're putting your *faith* (the title of this book!) in Jesus, then this is your story, too!

I WAS A MIDDLE SCHOOL DORK!
—KURT

As a middle schooler, almost every Saturday I'd go to the swap meet with a couple of friends. The swap meet was held in the parking lot of a local drive-in theater. At the swap, people at thousands of little booths were sold everything from sunglasses to surfboards to squirt guns to salt-and-pepper shakers. But on this particular Saturday we weren't there to buy something—we were there to *see* something! The week before we had walked by a big booth with a banner that read, COME AND SEE THE WORLD'S BIGGEST, MOST DISGUSTING RAT! (Girls, you have to trust me on this one...there isn't a middle school boy alive who doesn't want to take a peek at the world's biggest, most disgusting rat!) We couldn't see the world's biggest, most disgusting rat when we first saw the banner the week before because it cost $1 to see the world's biggest, most disgusting rat, and we had spent our last dollar on the world's biggest, most disgusting jawbreaker.

But this week we were back, each of us clutching a one-dollar bill and suddenly feeling a little nervous, knowing we were about to see the world's biggest, most disgusting rat! My friends chose me to go first. I gave the toothless worker my dollar and started to climb the ladder to peek into the cage. I got about halfway up and was paralyzed with fear. I suddenly realized I had lived 12 years without seeing the world's biggest, most disgusting rat, and I could probably live the rest of my life just fine without seeing it. Besides, what if the ladder wobbled and I fell in? What if I got trapped in the cage and became dinner for the world's biggest, most disgusting rat? I couldn't do it...and none of my friends could, either. Embarrassed, I asked the toothless worker if I could have my dollar back since I only went halfway up the ladder. He gave back half my dollar.

I'm 40 years old now, and I've still never seen the world's biggest, most disgusting rat.

SECTION 2

FAITH AND DOUBT

WHAT IS FAITH?

There's faith, and then there's *faith*. Let's explain: One use of the word *faith* describes a choice of religion or way of looking at God. For instance, there is the Mormon faith, the Jehovah's Witnesses faith, the Christian faith, and so on. Each of these faiths has its own understanding of God, the Bible, and spiritual stuff like that. Chances are, you identify yourself as part of the Christian faith, and either you or your parents bought you this book, *My Faith*, to help you understand more about it and how it applies to life as a young teenager. Since two Christians wrote this book, everything in here is from a Christian point of view.

A second use of the word *faith* actually relates to the one we just described...but goes further. *Faith* means believing and trusting in something even though you don't fully understand it, can't see it, and can't prove it completely. We believe in the Christian faith even though we don't understand everything about it, can't see everything about it, and can't prove it completely. Gosh, this sounds confusing! Here's an example that may help:

If you're like most people, you believe that we landed on the moon even though you don't fully understand everything about space travel. You believe we landed on the moon even though you didn't see it with your own eyes (sure, you've seen video footage, but that could be fake). You believe we landed on the moon even though you can't prove it completely; if some dude tried to convince you we never landed on the moon, you'd probably think he was wacky, and you'd most likely argue with him using your very limited moon knowledge as your weaponry. Even if he made some points, you would probably hold your ground. Sure, you may question a few things, but you would almost certainly walk away holding on to your belief that we did, in fact, land on the moon. Why? Because you have *faith* that we landed on the moon.

"DOES DOUBTING GOD MEAN I'M
NOT A GOOD CHRISTIAN?"

—TREVOR, EIGHTH GRADE

I (Kurt) have never been to Germany, but I have faith it exists. I have never met George Washington...I'm old, but not that old...but I have faith he was our first president. I've never touched a great white shark, but I have faith that I would get bitten if I tried. My faith in this stuff is built on lots of history, lots of other people's experiences, and lots of common sense.

You will never be able to prove everything about your Christian faith...and that's why it's called faith. However, your faith is built on lots of history, lots of proof, lots of other people's experiences, and lots of your own experiences, too.

HOW DO I GET MORE FAITH?

We used to think that if we tried hard enough (maybe with a little grunting!), we could *make* ourselves have more faith! But while it's true that we can *choose* to have faith (we choose every day to believe that Jesus' way of living is best), we can't really grow our own faith.

There's a really cool little verse in the Bible, in Deuteronomy 32:11. This is what it says:

...like an eagle that stirs up its nest

and hovers over its young,

that spreads its wings to catch them

and carries them on its pinions.

Cool, eh? Well, let's explain. God gave us this word-picture to help us understand our role and his role in how to grow our faith. In the picture, God is the mother eagle, and we're the baby eaglets.

Here's what happens. Baby eagles are hatched into a huge nest that the mom has lined with the softest feathers from her own body. Like the verse says, when it's time for the eaglets to learn to fly, the mom pulls up the big sticks from the nest, and they poke through the feathers. The babies get uncomfortable and are ready for change. Then the mom plops one of them on her back (called her "pinions") and takes them soaring through the sky! But just when the eaglet is thinking how cool it is to be flying high, the mom flips over and sends the baby falling toward the earth. Yikes! Do you ever feel like that? It's all part of God teaching us to have more faith! (A crash course, you might say...heh heh.)

But before the eaglet splats into the ground, the mom does something amazing: She dive-bombs down below the baby, and—this is the amazing part—she catches it on her back. Wow! After doing this a few times, the baby starts to spread its wings. But it still doesn't know how to fly. Now the mom flies just below and in front of the eaglet, and the wind coming off the back of her wings keeps the baby flying forward (rather than flying down!).

Can you see how this is a cool thing for us? Some of it is pretty uncomfortable—especially the falling part. But even the hard lessons are a part of God's great love for us. God wants us to have more faith, because he knows it's the best way for us to really experience a full and wonderful life.

So our choice—our role in getting more faith—is to ask God to give us more faith, and to be open to the process God wants to take us through.

MOSES' MOM AND FREAK-FAITH

Moses' mom was amazing! Her name (this is a good trivia question—your parents and youth workers probably won't even know the answer) was Jochebed.

Jochebed was a slave woman, living in Egypt (in the northeast corner of Africa). And just before baby Mo was born, the ruler of Egypt (called Pharaoh) decided there were too many Hebrew babies being born and ordered that all the Hebrew baby boys were to be killed! So when Jochebed found out she had a baby boy, she knew he would probably be found soon and killed. Can you imagine how awful that would be?

Jochebed must have felt like a free-falling baby eagle (see previous survival tip!). She had no options. And her only prayer must have been, "Please, God, let my baby live!" Then she took an almost-crazy step of faith. (You can read this story in Exodus 2:1-10.) She said to herself (well, something like this), "I don't see any options. And if God doesn't do something, then baby Mo will die for sure. So I'm going to take a risky step of faith and trust that God will come through with a solution."

Then she floated her kid by himself down a river.

Seriously! What a wacky idea! Jochebed took a basket, waterproofed it, plopped Moses in it, and sent him on a River Cruise for Babies.

Then the trippiest thing happened. Pharaoh's daughter was near the water a ways downstream when Mo-in-a-basket floated by. She ended up adopting him, paying Jochebed to raise him for a couple more years, and giving him the best education (in the palace!) that any kid could get (an education that wasn't available to *any* of the other Hebrew boys).

See, God loves providing wild solutions to our problems. And God answered Jochebed's prayers in an amazing way—way beyond what she could have imagined. But she took a risky, wild, gutsy, courageous step of faith first.

What problem do you have in your life right now? What risky step of faith could you take?

DOUBTS: WHY THEY'RE NORMAL

One day you're going through life, thinking everything's normal. You're good with God and all, and your beliefs in God-stuff seem rock solid. But then you hear from a teacher that a massive tsunami has killed tens of thousands of people on the other side of the world...and suddenly you're struggling with the belief you've always held that God is in control of everything.

Or your grandpa dies a long and painful death. And he was a really good guy. Suddenly you're not so sure about your long-held belief that "in all things God works for the good of those who love him" (Romans 8:28).

Or you have a really hard and super-important math test; you even study and work and prepare and get tutoring. And you pray and pray that God will give you a clear mind and help you remember how to do the problems. But you totally choke on the test and get a terrible grade. Suddenly you're not quite as sure about prayer as you were last week.

These are called doubts. Some Christians might tell you that you shouldn't have them. But that's not what the Bible shows us.

Doubts aren't only a *normal* part of being a middle schooler who's also a follower of Jesus—they're an *important* part. See, when you come into your middle school years, you already have some kind of faith decided—pre-teens are really good at coming to conclusions about things. But as a young teenager, you've been given a new way to think—it's part of growing up. And this new way of thinking means that stuff you thought you had all figured out will sometimes not make much sense anymore.

So doubts are good—as long as you don't hold on to them forever. Ask questions—of your parents, of your youth leaders, of God. Try to find new (and better!) answers to your faith questions. This is all part of growing into the faith and belief God wants you to have as a teenager.

DOUBTS: WHAT TO DO ABOUT THEM

Do you know what a doubt is? If you don't, it would be pretty helpful for you to go back and read the survival tip on the previous two pages before reading this one.

Okay. Now we're all on the same page. (Ha! No, really, we're all on this page!) Here's what you should do with your doubts...

Sooner or later, you'll probably think to yourself, *Self, I'm not sure I believe that anymore.* Or, *Self, I've believed this way about God for a long time, but it doesn't really make sense to me.* Or, *Wait, Self, how could that be true about God?* You get the idea. Then, immediately, as fast as you can, you'll run to the closet or basement or junk room (or wherever your family keeps empty boxes) and grab a box—just a small one, like a shoebox—and stuff that doubt in it. You'll yell at the box, "Take *that*, dirty ol' doubt!" Then never look at it or think about it again.

Except the problem with that "solution" (and while none of us would actually use a shoebox, many of us try to "stuff" our doubts by just ignoring them) is that it doesn't work! It's like stuffing too much grape jelly into a bag made of paper towels. It starts to, well, ooze. You don't want to ooze, do you?

So here's a better idea: Give your doubts the respect they deserve. Yeah, we know that sounds weird—so let us explain. Pretend a hungry lion escaped from a nearby zoo and was roaming around your schoolyard. It would be stupid to pretend the lion wasn't even there and just go on with your day. And it would also be stupid to run out and try to tickle the lion. Knowing that the lion could end your life in a second (or maybe two seconds), you'd give the lion the respect it deserves, right? Your doubts can destroy your faith if you completely ignore them, or if you focus on them too much.

So don't ignore your doubts. Bring them out into the open. You can do this by talking about them (though it's good to write about them and pray about them, too). Find an adult you really trust. Tell that person you want to talk about a doubt, and it's really important to you that they help you think about it, not just tell you to stop having the doubt (sometimes adults need that reminder).

God wants to help you work through your doubts, because having them, working through them, and eventually, moving past them, is all part of having a faith that survives middle school!

DOUBTS: HOW JESUS HANDLED THEM

You've probably heard the story of the disciple named Thomas, right? Don't worry if you haven't—we'll tell you! Poor Tom got the nickname "doubting Thomas" because of this story. But it's *such* a cool story of how Jesus handles doubts—both Thomas' *and* ours.

After Jesus rose from the dead and came out of the tomb, the disciples still didn't really understand what had happened. And they were afraid for their lives, hiding out in a locked room (you can read this whole story in John 20:24-31). Then suddenly Jesus was in the room. And they were, as you would expect, pretty pumped to see him.

But Thomas wasn't there. And when the rest of the disciples told Tom they'd seen Jesus, he didn't believe them, saying something like, "I won't believe it until I actually touch the nail holes in his hands and put my hand in the hole in his side where the soldier stabbed him to make sure he was dead."

A little while later, all the disciples were in the room again—and Thomas was with them this time. And Jesus showed up again. Now picture yourself as Thomas at this point. Don't you think seeing Jesus would have been enough? Thomas wouldn't have said, "Jesus, get over here—I need to touch those nail holes and put my hand in your side." But this is the cool part: Jesus helped Thomas process his doubt. Jesus didn't just let Thomas stuff his doubt in a box. He made Thomas come over and touch the nail holes and put his hand in the spear hole.

After all that, Jesus told Tom something like, "Okay, buddy, we've dealt with that doubt, and you can put it aside."

That's a great way to think about dealing with our doubts. Don't ignore them. Deal with them. Process them—with Jesus' help. Then, once you have a new understanding, once you've processed the doubt, set it aside. You don't have to keep returning to the same doubt over and over again (if you do, you probably never dealt with it in the first place).

CHILD*LIKE* FAITH AND CHILD*ISH* FAITH

In Matthew 19:13-15, Jesus talks about something you've probably heard before—how important it is for all of us (of any age) to have the faith of a child.

And in 1 Corinthians 13:11, Paul talks about how important it is to put childish thinking behind us as we grow up.

How do these two ideas fit together? It has to do with the difference between "child*like*" and "child*ish*." Those are two very different words, with very different meanings. *Childlike* means just what it says, "like a child." But *childish* means immature, like when you do something that would make sense if you were three (but, um, you're not three).

Child*like* faith, the kind that Jesus talks about, is pure faith. It means believing in Jesus without reservation. It's trusting that God really is who he says he is. It's being confident and sure about your beliefs so you act on them and live them out.

Child*ish* faith, on the other hand, is immature faith. It means settling for a three-year-old's faith when you're 12 (or 24, or 72).

God wants your faith and beliefs to grow with you. Even Jesus, when he was a young teenager, was described as growing in faith and knowledge. Of course there are things you now understand about math that you didn't understand when you were three. And there are things you now understand about *everything* that you didn't understand (or, you understood them differently) when you were knee-high.

The same is true of your faith. A three-year-old's faith won't get you very far with everything you know and understand about the world, now that you're becoming an adult. So allow your faith and understanding and beliefs to develop together. Choose to think about your beliefs. And ask God to help them get stronger.

UPGRADING YOUR OPERATING SYSTEM

You are at *such* a cool place in your faith development! See, when you go through your young teenage years (really, when you go though puberty, that time when your body and almost everything about you starts to drastically change into its more adult form), something amazing happens to your brain. It explodes! No, we're kidding...sort of.

You probably never realized it, but over the years of your short life, your brain has changed a bunch of times. Each time it changed, you had the ability to think in new and different ways. The last of these big changes in your brain happens about the time of your middle school years.

Here's the change: You get (or will get) the ability to think about thinking. Whoa! Is that confusing? Think of it this way: When you were younger, you were like a person living in a computer game that was a "first-person" game. You couldn't see yourself or think about how you fit into the world around you. You could only look out through your eyes and see (and think about) the world from that view. But this new thinking ability lets your brain switch between a "first-person" view and a "third-person" view (picture a video game where you can see your character moving around, not just looking out from your character's view). You can think about how you fit into the world around you, how others are seeing you, and other really deep things.

This has a *huge* impact on your faith! Here's another helpful example: The computer we're writing this book on (just like any computer you might use) has an operating system. And those operating systems get upgrades that make them work better and in new ways. So if you open up an old document that you made four years ago when your computer had an older operating system, your computer has to convert the file. You might make changes to the file, and when you go to save it again, the computer will ask you if you want to save it in the old operating system format, or in the new operating system format.

That's exactly what's happening in your faith development because of the very cool brain changes God has given you! Everything you understand about God and faith needs to be "upgraded" to your new operating system during the next few years. This is a big part of what causes doubts (ideas that your brain's old operating system thought up but that don't make enough sense to you anymore). Sometimes this can be hard work, or even frustrating. But it's a great thing, because it can leave you with a faith that will last a lifetime.

LEARN FROM DEMAS (ABOUT CHUCKING YOUR FAITH)

You probably haven't heard of Demas, a guy from the Bible. Let's change that.

You know how Jesus had disciples? They were a group of guys who followed him around, helped him with his work, and then carried on after Jesus went back to heaven.

Well, Paul (the guy who wrote most of the New Testament) had disciples, too. They're not as famous as Jesus' 12 guys. But Paul often mentions them at the end of the Bible books he wrote. Demas was one of Paul's disciples, and he's mentioned three times in the Bible.

The first two mentions don't tell us much (in Colossians 4:14 and Philemon 1:24). They just show us that Demas was with Paul for a long time—he traveled and hung out with Paul 24/7 for at least a couple of years. That would *have* to have a huge impact on anyone!

But the third time Demas is mentioned, it's not good news (in 2 Timothy 4:10). Paul says Demas deserted him (left him) because "he loved this world." That doesn't mean that Demas wanted to bring the story of Jesus to the people of the world because he loved them so much; it means that Demas chucked his faith—he chose to live a life with all the bad stuff that the world has to offer.

We don't know exactly what happened to Demas. But it seems that many people (especially teenagers) make choices like this. So many teenagers give up on really living for Jesus by the time they reach the end of their teenage years. We think the main reason for this—and the most likely reason for what happened to Demas—is simply the fact that living for Jesus isn't always easy (especially when you're a teenager). It means choosing *not* to do some things that many of your friends are doing. It seems Demas couldn't handle that. Can you? Is your faith strong enough?

WHAT IF I DON'T FEEL LIKE A CHRISTIAN?

BIBLE FACT: THE NUMBER OF NEW BIBLES DISTRIBUTED (SOLD OR GIVEN AWAY) IN THE U.S. EACH DAY: ABOUT 168,000.

Feelings are a really good thing! Just think how boring life would be without 'em. Without feelings, you'd never be excited, happy, sad, anxious, bored, or goofy. Without feelings, life would be missing most of what makes it so wonderful. However, there is one major problem with feelings: You can't always trust them.

Just because you feel something or don't feel something doesn't mean that particular something is or isn't true. You may have felt like the cute girl in your math class really liked you, only to find out she feels like you're a complete loser. Your feelings were wrong...she doesn't like you. Her feelings are wrong, too...you aren't a complete loser. You're just a normal guy who isn't liked by the cute girl (welcome to the club!).

There are probably times when you just don't feel like a Christian. Maybe you went to camp and felt super close to God, only to come home and feel far away from him. Maybe you've gone through a period of time when you read your Bible a lot and spent some good time alone with God, but you don't do that as much anymore. Maybe you've slipped back into some old habits or attitudes that you think a Christian wouldn't struggle with. Maybe you just don't *feel* like a Christian anymore. We've got good news! Whether you are or aren't a Christian has nothing to do with your feelings and has everything to do with facts.

It's a fact that Jesus died for you and kicked death's butt when he came back to life. It's a fact that Jesus offers a relationship with God and eternal life in heaven for those who believe in him. It's a fact that those who

do believe have been given a gift that can *never* be taken away. It's a fact that if you've accepted God's gift, then you're a Christian, whether you feel like it all the time or not. God's gift to you is just that—a gift! He gives it freely, and it's such an incredible gift that we can't possibly earn it. And once we've accepted it, that gift can never be lost—even if we feel like it has been.

SECTION 3

BIBLE STUFF

WHERE DID THE BIBLE COME FROM?

Did you know that the Bible is the most popular book in history? More copies of the Bible have been sold than any other book. It's an amazing book, one that's a whole lot different from any other. The normal steps to creating a book really aren't too tough: An author has an idea and gives his idea to the book company (called a publisher). The publisher then prints the book and delivers it to bookstores where people can buy it. There's a little more to it than that, but not much. But the Bible didn't get into your hands that way...it took a totally different path. In fact, that's part of what makes it such a cool book.

The best way to picture the Bible is to think of it as 66 individual books all bound together...sorta like a super-small, portable library! More than 40 different authors wrote these books (some wrote more than one), and it took about 1,500 years to complete! The Bible is broken into two main sections called the Old Testament and the New Testament. The OT talks a lot about God's original plan, how people have responded to him, and stuff like that. Most of the Bible stories you may remember from Sunday school come from the OT...stories like David and Goliath, Moses, Noah, and Daniel in the lions' den. The New Testament focuses more on Jesus, the beginning of the church, and how Christians should try to live. The writing of the Bible was complete about 100 years or so after Jesus was born. The men who wrote the Bible wrote what they saw and experienced and what the Holy Spirit was telling them to write.

In the early days, people would copy the entire Bible by hand just to get their own copy because there were no printing presses. In fact, that's what some people did all day, every day, just so more people could have a Bible! When the printing press was finally invented, guess what book was the first to be printed? Yep, the Bible.

> "MY YOUTH PASTOR IS ALWAYS SAYING HOW IMPORTANT THE BIBLE IS, BUT I DON'T KNOW VERY MUCH ABOUT IT."
> —SABRINA, SEVENTH GRADE

If you own a Bible, you own an incredible book, and it's worth reading.

HOW CAN I BE SURE THE BIBLE IS TRUE?

Okay, so the Bible is a popular book, and your grandma gave you one, and your youth pastor uses Bible verses at church...but is it true? Is it really *God's Word?* That's a fair question and a super-important one, too! Since the Christian faith is built on what the Bible has to say, it seems pretty important to know if it's true. In 2 Timothy 3:16, the Bible says that it's "God-breathed," which means the authors wrote down what they felt God was telling them to write. It also says to test stuff...that we shouldn't just believe what we hear. So it makes sense that we should test the Bible to see if it's really true, to see if it really was inspired by God. Here are a few examples of how people have put the Bible to the test:

Predictions in the Bible: The Bible includes more than 1,000 predictions, called prophecies, about things that are going to happen someday. Most of these have already come true. For example, the Old Testament is full of predictions about Jesus—like when he would be born, where he would be born, how he would die, and stuff like that. These predictions were written hundreds and hundreds of years before Jesus was ever born, and they all came true! There are some prophecies in the Bible that haven't happened yet, but since all the other prophecies have been proven true, it's safe to bet that the rest will come true, too.

Archaeology: Archaeology is the scientific word for studying the past based on stuff that was left behind. It's basically the science of digging for stuff to learn about history. Anyway, over the years, tons of stuff has been discovered that proves the Bible is true. Some people like to say that most of the events in the Bible never happened, that they were just made up, but archaeology has proved that these events are true.

People have died: That probably got your attention! Shortly after the life of Jesus, lots of the people who wrote books in the Bible were punished, tortured, and even killed by people trying to scare them into saying that it was all fake...that they made stuff up. The fact that people were willing to die for what they believed to be true is really impressive! Not too many people would die for something they knew was made up.

It's probably impossible to prove everything in the Bible is true, but it's also impossible to prove it's not, even though people have tried.

THE ROLE OF THE BIBLE

I (Kurt) consider myself a "thrower." What I mean is that I like to throw stuff away, to get rid of clutter, to toss things out that I haven't used in a while or that serve no purpose. Even though most people haven't thrown away their Bibles, they may as well have, because they never read them and probably don't see much use for them. Many people think of the Bible as a neat religious book that they should have around, but not as something that plays a role in their lives. So what's the Bible good for? Here are a few ideas:

The Bible is a map for our lives. Life is a road trip...one that's probably going to last 70 or 80 years! Along the way you'll find yourself in new territory, facing new challenges, and trying to figure out how to get to your final destination, whatever that may be. Wouldn't it be nice to have a map for the journey? You do...the Bible! The Bible is a map for your life. It's like a guidebook that helps you figure out the best route to take, make decisions, figure out what's right and wrong, and make the most out of the road trip called life.

The Bible helps us grow closer to God. The Bible is a letter from God to you. When you read it, you learn more about him and his love for you. The Bible helps us learn more about God and grow closer to him.

The Bible helps us grow closer to God *on our own.* Sure, you could rely on your youth pastor or parents to share stuff from the Bible with you, but why not read it on your own? Then it becomes much more personal and meaningful.

Think about it...God has given us a map for the road trip of life. It's not just a bunch of information, but God's very own ideas and wisdom and direction. You probably have lots of books sitting around your house that haven't been opened in years. Make sure the Bible isn't one of them!

COOL WAYS TO USE THE BIBLE (BESIDES JUST READING IT)

If you want to join your story with God's story (and we sure hope you do!), it kinda helps to actually *know* a bit about God's story. And the very best place—by far—to learn more about God's story is, of course, the Bible.

But maybe you hate reading. Or maybe you like reading but are ready to try something different. There are lots of other wonderful ways to connect with God's story in the Bible other than just reading it the regular old way. Here are a few things you could try:

Look for a promise, an example, or a warning. See if you can find one of these three things in a book of the Bible. They're not overly difficult to find because the Bible is full of 'em!

Think of how you would say it. Get a piece of paper or a computer keyboard and rewrite a Scripture passage in your own words. This really helps you understand what's going on in the passage because it makes you think through its deeper meaning.

Be a scribe. Before printing presses, the scribes copied Scripture, word by word, very carefully. God even commanded every new king of Israel to write out his own copy of the first five books of the Old Testament as his own personal copy. It's still a great practice—it helps you focus on what's actually written. Don't use a computer this time—just write it out in your own handwriting, old school!

Start with some psalms, or one of the shorter books in the New Testament.

Put yourself in a story. When you read a Bible story, put yourself in the story as one of the characters and try to think about it from that character's point of view. Try different characters—good ones and bad ones. This will give you a new way to connect with the amazing stories in the Bible.

Try *lectio divina*. (Say LEX-see-oh dih-VEE-nah.) This is a super-old way to read the Bible. It means "divine reading," and the idea is to read with your heart, not just your head. Here's how it works. Read a passage really slowly, letting the words soak in. Don't rush. Then read the passage again (still really slowly) and try to notice if any word or phrase catches your attention. If one does, stop reading and sit quietly for a while, letting that word or phrase roll around your brain. Ask God what he wants you to notice. What does he want to say to you? You might want to journal a bit, also.

BIBLE SAYINGS I'VE HEARD BUT MAY NOT TOTALLY UNDERSTAND: *SALT* AND *LIGHT*

Every now and then, the Bible will use some word-pictures or sayings to help us get a clearer picture of the truth God wants us to understand. They really do make a lot of sense, but sometimes at first glance, it's tough to figure out what they mean.

Here's one example: "You are the salt of the earth" (Matthew 5:13). Huh? What does that mean? Well, let's think about it: What do we know about salt? It's a mineral that adds flavor to things. Something bland like mashed potatoes suddenly becomes a bonanza of flavor for your taste buds when you add salt. Chances are, you like salted peanuts better than unsalted. How tasty would potato chips be without salt? Let's face it: Without salt the experience of eating would be a lot less exciting.

God wants his followers to be like salt. He wants us to be his seasoning to add flavor and excitement to the world around us. When we're added to the scene, things should be tastier (that's kinda weird, but you get the point). As Christ-followers, we should add some flavor to the world. The idea that church and Christianity are boring really doesn't make sense. God wants people to get a taste of the life he offers...a salty taste that leaves them wanting a little more.

The Bible also calls us "the light of the world" (verse 14). In a real way, people who don't know God are lost...kind of like when you're in the dark and can't find your way around. God wants us to shine brightly to our friends and family who don't know him.

> "I GUESS I DON'T READ THE BIBLE AS MUCH AS I SHOULD. IT'S JUST THAT I DON'T UNDERSTAND MOST OF IT!"
>
> —SPENCER, EIGHTH GRADE

When God's kids are salty, they add flavor to the world. When they let their light shine, they let others see God more clearly through them.

BIBLE SAYINGS I'VE HEARD BUT MAY NOT TOTALLY UNDERSTAND: *VINE AND BRANCHES*

Some things just work better when connected to something else. The steering wheel in a car works a whole lot better when it's connected to the front axle thingy that helps steer the car in the right direction. A kite works better when it's connected to a string. A blow-dryer works better when it's connected to an electrical outlet.

As our creator, God knows that people need to be connected in order to "work better," too. One of the reasons we have families and friendships is to help us connect with others. The Bible says that when God created Adam, he decided it wouldn't be good if Adam was alone—so he created Eve as a partner. And as important as friendship and family connections are, there's one connection that's even more important—a connection with God. If you've already read the chapter on creation, you'll remember that God created us to be in relationship with him. God knows that we work a whole lot better when we're connected to him.

In John 15:5 Jesus says, "I am the vine; you are the branches. If a man remains in me and I in him, he will bear much fruit; apart from me you can do nothing."

Think about this: *How well does a branch work if it isn't connected to the tree?* Sure, you can use it as a walking stick or toss it in the campfire, but the true purpose of a branch is to stay connected to the tree so it can grow, become strong, and produce more leaves and more fruit.

It's pretty much the same way with us. God wants us connected to him so we can grow stronger in our faith and live the lives he's planned for us.

MY FAITH

BIBLE FACT: THE EVENTS DESCRIBED IN THE BIBLE TOOK PLACE IN THE MIDDLE EAST. TODAY THESE LANDS ARE KNOWN AS ISRAEL, SYRIA, EGYPT, LEBANON, LIBYA, GREECE, JORDAN, ETHIOPIA, AND TURKEY. SEVERAL RIVERS AND MOUNTAINS STILL HAVE THE SAME NAMES THEY HAD DURING THE TIME JESUS WALKED THE EARTH.

BIBLE SAYINGS I'VE HEARD BUT MAY NOT TOTALLY UNDERSTAND: *THE GOOD SHEPHERD*

Salt and *Light*...those sayings make sense because we've all tasted salt, and we all have lights in our house.

Vine and branches...that saying makes sense because we've all seen branches—live ones connected to trees and dead ones that have fallen off.

But *The Good Shepherd*? None of us is a shepherd—well, okay, maybe one of you guys is a shepherd, which is a very cool, stinky, and odd thing for a middle schooler to be!

When Jesus calls himself *The Good Shepherd (John 10:11)* what does he mean? Let's look at some stuff we know about the relationship between a shepherd and his sheep.

First, a shepherd takes care of his sheep. Jesus wants to take care of us. *Second*, a shepherd protects his sheep. Jesus wants to protect us, too. *Third*, a shepherd gives his sheep guidance because they don't really know where to go on their own. Jesus wants to help guide us through life and get us where we're going. *Fourth*, a shepherd looks for the one that is lost. Jesus is on the lookout for us. When we wander off his path, Jesus notices, and he helps us get back on track.

Finally, a good shepherd...a really good shepherd... will even die for his sheep. Think about that. Instead of just saying, "You stupid sheep can worry about yourselves," or "Yikes—a wolf! I'm outta here!" A good shepherd will put the needs of the sheep first and even die for them if that's what it takes to protect them.

That's what Jesus did for us! The Bible says that he's our Shepherd—and not just any old shepherd, but a really good one. The best one ever. One who was willing to die for us, his sheep.

You see, sheep wouldn't last very long without a shepherd. They could wander around on their own, trying to take care of themselves and find their way back to safety if they ever got lost. Sure, they could probably do that on their own for a little while, but the lives of sheep are a whole lot better when there's a shepherd looking out for them!

A FEW BIBLE VERSES WORTH REMEMBERING

One of the best ways to grow in your friendship with God is to read the Bible and memorize some Bible verses. We couldn't think of a better way to end this book than to share some of our favorite Bible verses with you—ones we think are worth memorizing:

"For God so loved the world that he gave his one and only Son, that whoever believes in him shall not perish but have eternal life." John 3:16

"For the wages of sin is death, but the gift of God is eternal life in Christ Jesus our Lord." Romans 6:23

"For it is by grace you have been saved, through faith—and this not from yourselves, it is the gift of God—not by works, so that no one can boast." Ephesians 2:8-9

"I can do everything through him who gives me strength." Philippians 4:13

"If we confess our sins, he is faithful and just and will forgive us our sins and purify us from all unrighteousness." 1 John 1:9

"The thief comes only to steal and kill and destroy; I have come that they may have life, and have it to the full." John 10:10

"Don't let anyone look down on you because you are young, but set an example for the believers in speech, in life, in love, in faith and in purity." 1 Timothy 4:12

"For I am convinced that neither death nor life, neither angels nor demons, neither the present nor the future, nor any powers, neither height nor depth, nor anything else in all creation, will be able to separate us from the love of God that is in Christ Jesus our Lord." Romans 8:38-39

"A new command I give you: Love one another. As I have loved you, so you must love one another." John 13:34

I WAS A MIDDLE SCHOOL DORK!
—MARKO

Her name was Kathy, and I was convinced she was the most amazing girl ever. She'd just broken up with Jeff, big man on campus. But even though she was seriously out of my league, to my shock, rumor had it that she *liked* me!

Everybody told me I had to ask her to "go with me"—that's what we called it back then when you asked someone to be your girlfriend or boyfriend. (I didn't really understand why it was called that because we weren't going to "go" anywhere.)

So anyway, one night I was babysitting, and the little kids were all tucked in bed. It was time to call Kathy and pop the big question. So I called her, made small talk for a bit, and then said, "I have something to ask you." She waited. *And all that would come out of my mouth were little squeaky sounds!* I totally froze! So I hung up. Nice move, huh?

I dug around the family room cabinets in the house where I was babysitting and found a tape recorder (think old-fashioned: little tape cassette, clunky buttons, one tiny awful-sounding speaker). I practiced asking Kathy to "go with me" over and over, recording it so I could hear how each try sounded. After about 50 tries, it sounded perfect, and I was convinced I now had the courage (and the style, man!).

I called Kathy again, making up some lame reason for hanging up. Once again I said, "I have a question to ask you." Silence. Seriously, I thought I might have heard crickets chirping or something. I opened my mouth for the perfectly rehearsed, amazing performance. And once again—nothing but squeaky noises!

In my moment of panic, I did a very stupid thing. I grabbed the little tape recorder and held it up to the phone, and (yes, I really did) pushed "Play." But I'd forgotten to set the volume right, so my voice came out like I was screaming at her!

Anyhow, she said yes. And we "went together" for two weeks before she broke up with me and went back to Jeff, big man on campus. I don't know why—I bet he didn't even know how to use a tape recorder during a phone conversation!

SECTION 4

PRAYER

HOW TO PRAY

It's possible that most of us learned to pray the wrong way. When we were little, lots of us learned that praying was a lot like memorizing a nursery rhyme or rattling off a cute little poem. Some of us grew up only praying before dinner and at bedtime, and they were the same little prayers each time. They may have been something like this:

"Now I lay me down to sleep, I pray the Lord my soul to keep..." or *"God is great, God is good, thank you, God, for all this food."* Or the condensed version: *"God is neat, let's eat."*

The problem with prayers like these is that they tend to make prayer a meaningless little ritual...something we do out of habit even though it doesn't mean much to us. Prayer is our chance to communicate with God, our heavenly Father! He would love it if we got to know him better—and one of the best ways to do that is through prayer. But we can't really get to know him better and grow in our relationships with him if we always pray the same way and at the same time every day.

Think about your best friend. How weird would your friendship be if the only time you talked to him or her was at bedtime? You give her a call and say, *"Now I lay me down to sleep, you're a friend I think I'll keep,"* and then hang up the phone. You don't talk again until the next night: *"Now I lay me down to sleep..."* Not only would your friend think you were crazy, but she'd probably wonder how much her friendship really meant to you.

Prayer is your chance to talk to God, to share your life with him. It's your chance to connect with the Creator of the universe. God sees himself as your Friend, and he really wants your friendship to get better and better.

What's the right way to pray? It's simple. Just pray in a way that helps your friendship with God continue to grow—talk to him naturally, knowing he's right there by your side. The only wrong way to pray is if it's a meaningless, childish ritual.

OTHER WAYS TO PRAY

Just regular ol' talking to God is great. The only problem is that it *can* become pretty selfish sometimes—just about our big list of stuff we want to get from God. This is pretty normal, though; don't beat yourself up if your prayers are that way.

But at some point in your faith walk, you'll want to learn some *other* ways to pray. Here are a few you could try.

Keep a prayer journal. It can be really helpful to write your prayers. It's less like a conversation, sure, but it helps you to be more thoughtful. I (Marko) like to type prayers out on my laptop computer sometimes—just seeing the words on my screen really helps me focus on God and what I'm trying to say to him.

Pray with colors. Get some blank paper and some colored pencils or crayons or whatever. Spend a few minutes in silence, getting yourself quiet and thinking about God. Then express yourself to God through drawing. What you draw doesn't have to be an actual picture. It could be a symbol for something, or it could just be colors and textures that mean something to you (and that God will completely understand—remember, God knows everything).

Sit in silence. This one's tough. But if you learn how to do it, it can become one of your favorite ways to pray! See, usually our prayers are all about *us talking*. But God wants to talk to us, too, right? So how 'bout we give him a chance and just listen? If you do this, it's really important to find a quiet place without distractions. Get comfortable, sitting, and close your eyes. Focus on your breathing for a few minutes to get your attention, and ask God to speak to you. You might have a specific subject you want God to speak to you about, or you might leave it open. Then be quiet and wait. You may have a thought or a sense or an idea that you can tell came from God.

Pray "The Jesus Prayer." This is a simple prayer you can pray when you have no idea what else to pray. Jesus-followers have prayed this prayer for hundreds and hundreds of years! It's simply this: *Jesus Christ, Son of God, have mercy on me, a sinner.* The idea is to get quiet and calm and close your eyes (though this can be a cool prayer to do while you're walking, also, and you don't want your eyes closed then!). Make sure you're breathing normally and slowly. Then say (in your mind, not out loud) the first half of the prayer while taking a breath in, and the second half of the prayer while breathing out. It's the idea of breathing in Jesus, and breathing out our sin.

THE CHURCH AND WORSHIP

WHAT IS THE CHURCH?

Pretend you move into a new town by the beach, and at school one of your new friends invites you to church. Since your family is looking for a new church, you accept the invite.

"Great, I'll see you on Saturday at the pier," your friend says.

"Your church is called The Pier?" you ask. "And you meet on Saturday?"

Your new friend laughs and says, "Our church isn't called The Pier; we meet at the pier each Saturday to surf, hang out, and share some food. We usually end up talking about God and sharing some prayer requests at the end."

Believe it or not, your new friend has just invited you to church. Sure, it's a little different from the church you're used to...no building, no Sunday school—in fact, no Sunday anything! But maybe there's something more to church. Maybe the church isn't just a building. Maybe the church is supposed to be more than a bunch of people sitting together on a Sunday morning on really uncomfortable chairs, singing a few songs, and listening to a sermon. Maybe what your friend invited you to is actually a better example of what the church is supposed to be!

The church isn't only a formal gathering of Christians on Sunday. The church is made up of all believers in Jesus. Us, you, the Christians in China, the Christians in Iraq...together, we make up the church. And as *the church*, we're a whole lot more effective when we aren't huddled in a building, singing songs. If you take the time to read the first couple of chapters in the book of Acts in the Bible, you'll get a pretty cool picture of what the church looked like in the beginning. It was just a bunch of Jesus-followers who lived life together, shared what they knew with others, and gathered together often to learn more and be encouraged.

> "MY FRIEND ASKED ME WHAT CHURCH WAS. ALL I COULD THINK TO TELL HIM WAS THAT CHURCH IS WHERE I GO ON SUNDAYS."
>
> —MICHAEL, SEVENTH GRADE

We both go to church almost every week and think you should, too. It's important to have a place to get together with other Christians to grow in our faith and encourage each other.

But it's just as important to remember that the church isn't just something you go to one day a week; it's something you're a part of every day of the week!

DO I HAVE TO GO TO CHURCH TO BE A CHRISTIAN?

How many times have you argued with your mom or dad because it was time to go to church, and you didn't want to go? You may need to go to the junk drawer in your kitchen and grab a calculator to add it up! We're both pastors, and we both have middle school daughters. Both of the youth groups that our daughters go to are pretty fun. They aren't perfect, but they aren't a bad place to go if you're in middle school. We have all these things going for us, and guess what? Our girls still argue with us about going to church sometimes! They like church, but sometimes they'd rather sleep in.

A question they've both asked may be the same one you've asked: "Do I have to go to church to be a Christian?" We've got really good news for you. No, you don't have to go to church to be a Christian. Going to church isn't what makes you a Christian. (Standing in a garage doesn't make you a car, does it?)

A Christian isn't somebody who goes to church. A Christian is somebody who has accepted God's gift of forgiveness through Jesus. It's that simple.

So why go to church? There are lots of reasons to go to church. Here are a few to get you thinking:

- Going to church helps me learn more about God and grow closer to him.

- Going to church helps me stay connected to other Christians.

- Going to church encourages me.

- Going to church helps show God that he's important to me.

- Going to church gives me a chance to use my gifts and talents to glorify God.

- Going to church reminds me that I'm not alone... that there are other people walking God's path.

- Going to church helps keep my parents off my back. That's not a very spiritual reason, but it's true!

All the stuff we just listed is really helpful stuff. It's all stuff that God wants us to experience. Can we experience them without church? Maybe, but your church is there to help!

WHAT DO THESE WORDS MEAN?

If you go to church or come from a Christian family, you've probably heard some of these words. We've tried to define them in a way that hopefully makes sense:

Repentance: This word has been around a long, long time. In the church, *repentance* means to recognize you've done something wrong and ask for forgiveness. It also means to turn away. A common church saying is "to repent of your sins." To sin means doing wrong in God's eyes. When you repent of your sin, you recognize that what you did was wrong, ask for forgiveness, and turn away from that sin.

Sanctification: This is a fancy word describing our experience of growing closer and closer to God. Growing in our faith is a process that happens slowly over time. As Christians, we should try to be as much like Jesus as we can be. Becoming more and more like Jesus is called *sanctification.*

Grace: *Grace* is getting something good, for free, that we don't deserve. We don't really deserve a relationship with God or his gift of heaven, but he gives it to us because of his grace. When Jesus died on the cross for us, it was an act of grace. We didn't deserve it, but he did it for us anyway.

Sacraments: If you've taken communion or been baptized, you've participated in a sacrament. A *sacrament* is an outward action that shows your inward desire to grow closer to God. There are other sacraments, but baptism and communion are two of the more common ones.

Salvation: Being saved, or *salvation*, is what happens when someone trusts Jesus and accepts his gift of forgiveness. You may have heard somebody say, "I was saved when I was 15 years old." In other words, that person became a Christian at 15.

Reconciliation: This is a big word that could be the most important word in the Christian faith. Remember, God's original plan was to have a relationship with us, his creation. But our sin separates us from God. Because of sin, our relationship with God is broken and needs fixing...the mess needs to be cleaned up! *Reconciliation* means repairing the relationship...making things right. The only way our relationship with God can be fixed is by putting our trust in Jesus. Jesus provides reconciliation between God and people. He cleans up the mess!

WHAT IS WORSHIP?

If we asked *you* this question, we're pretty sure you'd give some form of the answer we hear from middle schoolers all the time: Singing to God. But that's only *one way* of worshiping God, and it might not even be worship, depending on you!

Do you know what it means to acknowledge someone? It means to notice they're there and give them your attention. Well, worship is really us acknowledging God. It's when we say, "God, I'm going to focus on you now, I'm going to say stuff that's true about you, and I'm going to talk about how amazing you are." Think of a scene from a movie where a guy is trying to express to a girl how amazing she is: "Your eyes, they're like two little pools of deep water; and when you speak, I feel like I'm floating in the air, spinning around; and your breath smells like honey, straight from the clover." Okay, give us a moment to hurl. But really, that's what worship is.

So *sometimes* we worship with singing (most of us are used to this because our churches call the Sunday meeting a "worship service"). But there are lots of ways to worship God. Prayers can be worship (especially if they're prayers about how awesome God is).

But here's the really big-deal survival tip: *The worship that God really digs, so much more than our singing or anything else, is when we worship him with our lives.* The Bible says in a bunch of places that the kind of worship God *really* wants is when we notice other people's needs and take care of them.

Are you a worshiper of God? It's not a Sunday-morning-singing thing only! Worshiping God is an everyday thing, acknowledging him as the God of all creation, 24-7!

COMMON QUESTIONS
ABOUT CHRISTIANITY

AREN'T ALL RELIGIONS BASICALLY THE SAME?

We've both worked with middle school students a long time, and this question is one that we've heard over and over again. It's a good question. One that deserves an answer: NO! Now, that may sound a bit harsh, but it makes total sense when you stop to think about it.

Almost nothing in this world is "all the same." When you go to Baskin-Robbins to get ice cream, the flavors aren't all the same. You have 31 different types of ice cream to choose from! Starbucks sells all kinds of coffee. You can get a one-dollar cup of plain ol' stuff or pay five dollars for one with mocha, caramel, and whipped cream. Try going to a bike shop and saying, "I'd like to buy a bike, please. Any bike will do since they're all the same." The mullet-headed, nose-pierced, bike-shop-owner dude would look at you as if *you* looked weird or something.

Religions aren't all the same, either. They may have some things in common, but they aren't all the same. Some of the ways religions are different from each other include what they teach about God, what they teach about Jesus, what they teach about getting to heaven, and what they teach about the Bible. There are other differences, but those are the biggies.

Another question we hear a lot is, "Are all religions true?" Again, another good question that deserves an answer: NO!

The reason all religions can't be true isn't just because they're different. Different types of coffee are still true coffees, and different ice cream flavors are still true ice creams. The reason all religions can't all be true is because they all hold different beliefs that they claim as truth...beliefs that are totally opposite from each other. If beliefs about the same thing are opposite from each other, they can't both be true.

> "ALL RELIGIONS ARE PRETTY MUCH
> THE SAME, RIGHT?"
> —ALLIE, EIGHTH GRADE

A simple example is how somebody gets to heaven. Christianity says that heaven is a free gift. Many other religions believe a ticket to heaven must be earned. Christianity believes that the gift of heaven is given to us through Jesus, God's Son. Many other religions believe that Jesus was a good guy but wasn't God's Son and has nothing to do with heaven. How can both be true?

Another difference between Christianity and other religions? Christianity isn't just a religion. Most religions make a big deal out of making sure you say the right stuff, do the right stuff, and stay away from the wrong stuff. Most religions focus on looking good on the outside. And while Christianity holds outward behavior as important, it's not the most important thing—it's about friendship with Jesus. And a true friendship with Jesus doesn't have a whole lot in common with religion.

WHAT'S THE TRINITY ALL ABOUT?

Have you ever tried to explain something but didn't quite know how? That's how we feel about this little chapter on the Trinity. The Trinity is hard to explain. It's almost unexplainable! Trying to explain it is a lot like trying to explain geometry...it's possible, but really hard for most people!

Let's take a look.

The word *Trinity* isn't mentioned in the Bible, but Bible scholars and other really smart people came up with that word to help describe God.

God is made up of three persons: the Father, the Son (Jesus), and the Holy Spirit. These three persons of God are called the Trinity. The Father is not the same person as the Son; the Son is not the same person as the Holy Spirit; and the Holy Spirit is not the same person as the Father. They are completely separate from each other, but they are all the same God. See how easy that is? Uh, okay, let us give you four examples that don't totally explain the Trinity but will help give you a better idea of how it may look:

An egg: There are three parts to an egg: The yolk, the white, and the shell. Each part is its own separate deal, but together they make a complete egg.

An apple: An apple has skin, a core, and flesh. Each part is unique, but each part is equally important.

Water: Water exists in three forms: liquid, solid (ice), and gas (steam). Each form of water is different, but each is still completely water.

A triangle: A triangle consists of three equal sides. Each side exists on its own, but each side is also part of the whole triangle.

Every once in a while you will come across things in your Christian faith that are really hard to figure out. There are just some things that don't have super-easy answers and explanations. And guess what? That's okay! The Bible doesn't really have a whole lot to say about the Trinity, but it does point to the Trinity as a picture of who God is. God is the Father, the Son, and the Holy Spirit.

HOW CAN GOD BE EVERYWHERE AND KNOW EVERYTHING?

Wouldn't it be cool if you could be everywhere at once? Now, if you combined that with the ability to know everything about everything, you would be a true-life superhero! Sadly, you're a mere human being, and obstacles like time and space limit you.

But God does know everything. Yes, everything. And God is everywhere at once. That's right. If you're reading this book in Kansas, he's there. If you're reading this book in Hawaii, he's there, too. In fact, he's probably catching a few waves!

There's an old church song that talks about God holding the whole world in his hands. It's a song that came from the Bible.

> *In his hand are the depths of the earth,*
> *and the mountain peaks belong to him.*
> (Psalm 95:4)

How is that possible? How can God be everywhere and know everything? Well, the reason is the same reason we can't. Remember, we are limited by natural laws that God put into place when he created the universe—laws that limit some of our abilities as humans. We can't be everywhere at once because of the law of space. We don't know everything because of the law of time (we don't know what's going to happen tomorrow because the law of time won't let us travel to tomorrow). But those laws don't limit God. Since God is the creator of time and space, he lives outside their boundaries. We are limited by time and space, but God isn't.

Okay, time for a few new words to amaze your friends!

Omnipresent (say om-knee-PREZ-ent): *The ability to be everywhere at the same time.* Only God is omnipresent because only God lives outside the boundaries of space.

Omniscient (say om-NISH-ent): *The ability to know everything about everything.* Only God is omniscient because only God lives outside the boundaries of time.

You don't need to make an appointment with God. He's with you all the time, and he knows what tomorrow looks like!

IF GOD IS SO GOOD, WHY IS THERE SO MUCH BAD STUFF?

You would think that life works something like this: God creates people...God loves people...only good things happen to people since God loves them.

God could totally make life work like that. But for some reason life works like this instead: God creates people...God loves people...bad things happen to people even though God loves them.

If bad things are going to happen, shouldn't they just happen to the people who don't love God back? Why in the world would God let bad things happen to good people, people who love him back? If God really loves us, why would he let bad things happen? Why would he let a little baby get a serious disease? Why would he let millions of people in other countries go without enough food? Why would he let a teenager die in a car crash?

Are you ready for this? All this bad stuff is actually a result of the fact that God loves us a whole lot! Right now you may be thinking, *Marko and Kurt, I thought you guys were just plain old...now I think you guys are old and stupid!* Let us explain.

When God created Adam and Eve, he loved them very much, and his hope was that they would choose to love him back and obey him. He gave them total freedom in the Garden of Eden with only one rule: Don't eat from that tree over there. He loved Adam and Eve so much that he didn't want to force them to obey him; he wanted to let them choose.

They chose to disobey God. This choice was the first sin, and it opened the door for all the sin and bad stuff that has happened since. In a way God said, "Now that you've chosen to disobey me and sinned , I'm going to allow stuff to happen that wouldn't have happened before." Once sin entered the world, it caused all sorts of bad stuff, like sickness, and crime, and even death. This is why we need reconciliation with God through Jesus (remember when you read about that a few chapters ago?).

> "I JUST DON'T GET WHY THERE'S SO MUCH
> BAD STUFF IN THE WORLD."
> —AUTUMN, SIXTH GRADE

God loves you very much! Being a Christian doesn't mean bad things won't happen, but it does mean that God will be with you when they do.

SPIRITUAL GROWTH

HOW CAN I GROW IN MY FAITH?

God wants you to keep growing. We're not talking about growing taller, smarter, stronger, or better looking! That kind of growth is all fine, but there's a type of growth that's much more important: Growing in your Christian faith and your friendship with Jesus.

Physical growth doesn't happen automatically—there are some things that need to happen, like eating. You grow stronger by working out. You grow smarter by reading and learning. Almost all growth requires some sort of effort—it doesn't happen automatically.

It's the same way with our Christian faith. God wants us to grow in our understanding *of* him, our commitment *to* him, and our friendship *with* him—but it won't happen automatically. It takes a little effort. There are all kinds of ways to grow in your faith. It's important to realize that God doesn't have some sort of checklist to see if we're doing the right things. He doesn't have some secret handshake or code we have to crack in order to grow closer to him. He's created us all differently, and there are lots of different things that help us grow in our faith. Here are a few ideas to get you started:

Read the Bible. You probably guessed this would be first on our list! Reading your Bible really is an important way to grow in your faith because it tells us everything we need to know about God and how to live life with him.

Read other Christian books. Congratulations, you're doing this right now, and look how much you've grown! There are all kinds of books to help you understand the Bible and grow in your friendship with God.

Talk to God. Make a habit of spending some alone time with God. Praying and talking to God helps you grow closer to him.

> "I LIKE THE IDEA OF GROWING CLOSER TO GOD, BUT I'M NOT SURE HOW I'M SUPPOSED TO DO THAT. I CAN'T EVEN SEE GOD; HOW AM I SUPPOSED TO GROW CLOSER TO HIM?"
>
> —BRIANNA, SEVENTH GRADE

Stay connected to other Christians. Having a tight group of Christian friends at church or at school is a great way to help you grow. Good Christian friends can encourage you and challenge you to keep growing.

Have some non-Christian friends, too. How will they ever hear about Jesus if all the Christian kids huddle together all the time? Besides, nothing helps you grow in your faith like sharing it with someone else.

Serve. Volunteer in the children's ministry at your church. Tutor a younger child after school. Go on a mission trip.

Your faith—your friendship with Jesus—is meant to be an exciting, living, growing adventure! Give it a try.

WHERE CAN I FIND GOD?

Let's say you meet someone at school who you think would make a really good friend. What do you do? How do you pursue that friendship? Well, of course, the *main* thing you have to do is spend time with that person because friendships grow over time as we spend time together.

The same is true with God. If you want to have a close relationship with God (which, by the way, God really wants!), you have to spend time with him. Makes sense, doesn't it?

So where can you find God to spend time with him?

The first and most obvious answer is through the Bible. Remember, the Bible isn't like any other book. We call it "the living Word of God" because the Bible's words help you actually meet up with God—the Bible is full of inspiration and great ways to draw closer to him.

But there are other places to "find" God, because he is—after all—totally present, all around us. The trick is to be open to where God shows up for you. If you'll listen and look, you'll find God ready to speak to you through music (God digs music!). And you'll find God through art. And you can really find God through the beautiful nature he created. You can find God through other people who have Jesus living in them (again, makes sense, doesn't it?).

And—this is a biggie—you can find God through prayer. When you talk to God, he listens. It's a *huge* promise in the Bible. And this is a little harder: When you quiet yourself down, get rid of distractions, and ask God to speak to you, God (through the Holy Spirit) will show up in your thoughts and dreams.

Here's a faith survival tip: *Watch and listen for God all over the place.* The more time you spend with him, the more your relationship with him will grow. And the more your relationship with God grows, the more your life will have meaning and purpose.

PLAYING IT SAFE = A STUPID, BORING LIFE

All through the Bible we read about people who missed out on things that could have been the most amazing experiences of their lives:

- The disciples who sat in the boat watching while Peter jumped out and walked on the water toward Jesus.

- The Hebrew fighting men who wouldn't battle Goliath and instead watched as a little kid named David killed him.

- Demas, Paul's disciple, who left Paul because his priorities were all jacked (if you don't know this story, check out page 54).

And so many more!

Here's the question you need to ask yourself: *What kind of life do I want to have?* And if your choices are A) an amazing life full of excitement, adventure, meaning, and satisfaction, or B) a wimpy, boring, super-dull life that's pretty much a waste of oxygen, uh, we're confident you'd pick the first one. Please...you did, right? Okay, good.

Here's how it works: The *only* way to really experience the best life (that doesn't mean the *easiest* life, by the way), is to live completely for Jesus. Remember—Jesus invented us! Since he knows us better than anyone else—even better than we know ourselves—he's the only one who really knows what "the best life" really looks like for us.

So if you play it safe and only look out for yourself, or if you don't trust God and live the way he tells us to live, you're robbing yourself of the best life possible. And that's pretty stupid, isn't it?

Here's a faith survival tip: Don't just play around at being a Jesus-follower. Choose to be courageous in living the life Jesus wants for you!

HOW TO BE THE COOLEST TRANSFORMER

When you were younger, we bet you had a Transformer. Or even if you didn't have one, you played with one at a friend's house. Or at the very least you saw them on TV and really wanted one!

Transformers were those little plastic play characters with moving parts. It'd start as one thing—like a tiger, or a robot, or a normal-looking dude. But when you spun this part around and twisted that part and flipped that thing over and lifted those two things up...*then* it *transformed* into a flying, fighting superhero that shot rockets out of a backpack. Or something like that.

Well, here's the dealio. If you're a follower of Jesus, *you are* a transformer! Seriously! Second Corinthians 5:17 says, "Therefore, if anyone is in Christ, he is a new creation; the old has gone, the new has come!"

See? Jesus is transforming you—making you better! We don't know about you, but we can guess that you're enough like us—and we're pretty stoked about the idea of being made new...because we know ourselves just well enough to know that we're dirtbags. I mean, we're good guys and all—we're nice enough to people, especially if they're nice to us. But deep down, in our most secret places...well, let's just say you don't want to go there!

So we think being re-made into something new, something better (ooh, wait—that should be some*one* new, some*one* better!) is a pretty great deal. We'll take it!

Here's a survival tip for ya: *Invite Jesus to "go for it" in the process of transforming you!*

HOW'S YOUR REFLECTION?
(REFLECTING JESUS)

You gotta check out this story in Exodus 34:29-35. Moses, the guy God used to lead the Hebrew people out of slavery in Egypt, had a glow-in-the-dark face!

See, Moses was one of the few people in the history of the world who got to meet with God in person. I mean, you and I can meet with God every day—God wants to have that kind of real and everyday relationship with us. But when Mo met with God, God was physically there (somehow, we don't totally understand that). And because God is pure holiness, pure goodness, his "glory" is like light—really powerful light...so powerful, in fact, that God couldn't subject too much of his presence on ol' Mo—just God's back as he passed in front of Mo, believe it or not!

Then after Mo met with God, Mo's skin glowed. It totally freaked out the Hebrew people. So Mo started wearing a veil over his face. But every time he went to meet with God again, he'd come out with the shiny face.

Now check this out, because it's way cool. We get something so much better than a shiny face! I mean, it would be kinda cool to have a glow-in-the-dark face like Mo did. But what we get is better.

In 2 Corinthians 3:12-18, Paul talks about Mo's shiny face. And he says that we don't have to worry about our faces fading like Moses' did. In verse 18, Paul writes, "And we, who with unveiled faces all reflect the Lord's glory, are being transformed into his likeness with ever-increasing glory, which comes from the Lord, who is the Spirit."

We get to have our entire *lives* transformed—changed! That's *way* better than getting a glow-in-the-dark face!

So the faith survival tip of the day: *Are you reflecting Jesus with your whole life?*

HOW TO BOUNCE BACK WHEN I'VE MESSED UP

Paul, the guy who wrote most of the New Testament, writes that he has a hard time doing what he knows is the right thing to do and that he usually ends up doing the wrong thing—the thing he knows he shouldn't do. He doesn't share details about the stuff he did, but he admits he made mistakes. Paul, a man God used to change the world, messed up...he messed up *a lot*!

You might be the world's greatest middle school student. You may go to church every week, do your homework on time, and help little old ladies cross the street. But because you're human, you're going to mess up. You're going to make some honest mistakes and some not-so-honest mistakes. There are going to be things that you know you shouldn't do, but you will choose to do them anyway. Guess what? That doesn't make you a bad Christian; it just means you're normal—and unfortunately, sinning is normal. So how do you bounce back after you've messed up? We've listed a few tips below that can help. They aren't step-by-step instruction manuals—just a few ideas that may help you get back on track next time you mess up:

Admit the mistake. Way too many people try to pass the blame. They blame anybody and anything except themselves. An important part of bouncing back is being willing to admit when you've made a mistake.

Make it right. Then look for a way to correct the problem. If you hurt somebody's feelings, gossiped about a friend, held a grudge, or disobeyed your parents, go to those people and apologize. This step is really important for the stuff you have purposely done that you know you shouldn't have. Then confess your sin to God and ask his forgiveness.

Fail forward. This is an old saying that means when we fail, we can either let the failure keep us down, or we can learn from it and move forward, becoming stronger than we were before. Everybody fails! We all mess up. The key to bouncing back after a mess-up is to learn from our mistakes and move forward.

Remember that God loves you 100 percent. The Bible says that nothing can separate us from God's love. That means God loves you just as much in the middle of your mess-up as he did before it happened.

WHAT DIFFERENCE DO MY FRIENDS MAKE?

A couple of years ago a buddy of ours was hanging out and talking with a large group of students. He said, "If you want to know what you will be like in 10 years, just take a look at the type of people you choose as friends, because you'll turn out like the people you hang out with." To prove his point he tried a little experiment. He asked everybody to separate into groups with their closest friends. In a matter of seconds, the group was split into a bunch of little clusters of friends. The experiment continued. "Now, choose somebody in your group to take some notes," he said. "As a group, make notes about the types of clothes you're wearing, the kinds of music you enjoy, how you spend your free time, and stuff like that." After about 10 minutes, he asked for a brief report from each group of friends, and the results were really interesting. The students discovered that they had a whole lot in common with their friends. They dressed alike, enjoyed the same music, and had similar hobbies. In fact, they discovered that the closer their friendship with someone was, the more alike they were!

The truth is that friends rub off on each other. Your attitudes, opinions, hobbies, interests, and all that stuff rub off on your friends, and theirs rub off on you. The result: The longer you're friends with someone and the closer the friendship is, the more alike you become! This is a super-important fact of life because it proves that the old guy knew what he was talking about: *We become like the people we hang out with.* The Bible tells us, "He who walks with the wise grows wise, but a companion of fools suffers harm" (Proverbs 13:20). It's not just the Bible, youth pastors, and your parents who think this is important. Movie star Will Smith says, "You are who your friends are."

> "I REALLY LIKE MY FRIENDS! I FEEL LIKE I CAN TRUST THEM."
> —BRETT, EIGHTH GRADE

That's why who you choose as your closest friends is crucial. Your friends will play a big role in your growth as a Christian. They will either help your growth, or they will hurt it. This doesn't mean you shouldn't have friends who aren't Christians, but it does mean you want to have *some* close friends who are also trying to grow closer and closer to God.

Take a look at your closest friends. You are becoming more and more like them every day. Do you like who you're becoming?

I WAS A MIDDLE SCHOOL DORK!
—KURT

When I was in middle school, my friend Jaime and I walked home from school every day. On the way home we'd pass a Taco Bell, and the smell of warm bean and cheese burritos was always too good to pass up—for Jaime. (My family was pretty poor, and luxuries like Taco Bell were out of the question.) Jaime always had money, and he always wanted to stop at Taco Bell. As a result the same thing happened over and over again, almost every day.

We'd go into Taco Bell, and Jaime would pull out a ton of money and buy himself a couple of burritos. I would ask Jaime if he'd buy me one, and his response was *always* the same: "I won't buy you a burrito, but I will give you a nickel." The dude had 20 bucks in his pockets, but he'd only give me a nickel! I would always accept his nickel, though, because for a nickel I could buy a warm tortilla. Then I'd take the warm tortilla and squeeze a packet of hot sauce into it. The result: A warm burrito with everything except the meat, beans, and cheese! It was totally embarrassing! Jaime and I would continue our walk home...him munching on a couple of burritos, and me munching on a tortilla filled with hot sauce. Deep down I knew Jaime thought it was fun to watch me ask the lady at the counter for a five-cent tortilla, and deep down, the whole process felt embarrassing. But for some reason, Jaime and I went through the whole routine over and over again all through middle school.

What's the point of this story? I dunno...I guess it's just a reminder that middle school can be a really weird time of life.

A FEW BIBLE PEEPS

JAEL AND TOUGH STUFF

One of our favorite faith stories in the Bible is of an amazing woman named Jael (say jay-EL). You can find her whole story in Judges 4:14-22. But here's a summary:

Jael was a tent-wife (like a housewife, but she lived in a tent). The Hebrew people were at war with another country, but Jael was part of neither group. The two main general dudes were Barak (head of the Hebrew army, pronounced buh-RACK) and Sisera (head of the opposing army, pronounced SIS-ser-uh). During battle, God was helping the Hebrew army to win, and Sisera, in one of the wimpiest moves in history, ran away on foot! Barak chased after him.

Can you picture this? One general chasing another—no horses, no chariots, no guards. So Sisera stumbled, worn out and tired, into the little camp where Jael's tent was. She was there alone (it's not clear why, but her husband—and everyone else—wasn't there). Sisera ordered Jael to hide him.

Jael seemed to have known that God was asking something big of her, so she turned into an award-winning actress, offering Sisera a comfy little pile of furs to lie on and hide under. And when he asked for water, she made it a little better and brought him milk and cookies (well, not cookies, but milk and some goodies). Then Sisera fell asleep.

Okay, here's where the story gets a bit ugly. Ready? Jael picked up a big ol' tent peg and a hammer and went to where Sisera was sleeping. And Jael pounded the tent peg through his head (through his temple—the soft spot on the side of your head next to your eyes) and into the ground. Barak showed up, but only to find Sisera dead, pegged to the ground!

Now remember, Jael was a tent-wife—*not* a warrior-woman! Pounding tent pegs through generals' heads was not something she did every day, and we're sure it totally weirded her out!

Sometimes following God requires tough stuff of us. That doesn't mean you need to start nailing tent pegs through people's heads! But it might mean some other tough stuff, like telling the truth when it's difficult, or being nice to someone who's mean to you, or choosing to not go along with the crowd even when you'll be teased.

Is your faith strong enough for the tough stuff?

SAMSON AND SPIRITUAL PRIORITIES

Samson had *issues.* Seriously!

Samson had this amazing and wild deal going with God. He committed himself to living his whole life for God, and as a sign of this commitment, he promised to never cut his hair. Sam was the original longhaired freak. And the other side of the deal? God gave Sam superhuman strength (really, like, you *have* to read some of his wild stories in Judges 14 and 15).

So Samson was going through life like a pro wrestler, doing his superhuman, superhero-strength things but staying focused on his commitment to God. And then...Delilah (say deh-LIE-luh).

Delilah was a hottie, a teaser, and a bit of a bad girl thrown in the mix. Sam got seriously sideways when he met Delilah—he couldn't think straight anymore. And he started to have that massive desire to be with her all the time.

Delilah didn't give a rip about Samson but saw a way to make money off the fact that he was so head over heels for her. There were bad guys who wanted to know the secret of Samson's strength so they could stop him or kill him. So Delilah took money from these guys to find out.

Three times—*three times!*—she begged and whined and teased and pleaded with Samson to tell her his secret (it's championship-level whining—you can read about it in Judges 16). The first two times Samson lied, giving some silly ideas, like tying him up with new strings that had never been used and such. And each time, the bad dudes came in to ambush him, only to have him kick their booties.

But the third time—*the last time!*—Samson gave in to Delilah and told her the secret of his commitment-honoring long hair. When he was asleep, Delilah cut off his hair and called in the bad dudes. Samson got his eyes plucked out and was put into manual labor like an animal.

There's a *huge* lesson in here for us. Samson gave up his long-term goals (of serving God, of being 100 percent committed to God) to satisfy his short-term desires ("Ooh, Delilah, you're so sexy"). We do the same thing all the time—maybe not for Delilah, but for other things we want to do or say or own or experience, even though those things don't match up with who we really want to be in the long run.

Don't be a Samson. Make decisions based on your long-term goal of living for God!

PETER AND STEPPIN' OUT

Peter is the coolest! Yeah, he messed up all the time (like the time he cut a guy's ear off, and Jesus had to stick it back on the guy's head!). Peter was a big-time "act first, think later" kind of guy. But we (Marko and Kurt) are kinda like that—so we like Petey.

But there's one story where Peter's hero status really shines out—though lots of people miss it. It's the story where Jesus walked on the water. Heard that one? *Especially* if you haven't read it, you should check it out in Matthew 14:22-33.

The disciples were in a boat in the middle of the night, and the wind and waves were too much for them (even though a bunch of them were fisher-men and were really good with boats), and they couldn't get the boat back in to shore. At about three in the morning, they saw this human-like shape walking toward them on top of the water (remember, it was stormy—Jesus wasn't just glid-ing along a still surface!). And the disciples totally freaked out—"It's a ghost!"

Jesus yelled to them, "Dudes, chill! It's me, Je-sus!" (Or something like that.) But the disciples weren't sure if they could trust the voice—I mean, what if it was a ghost just *saying* it was Jesus? So good ol' Petey got to the edge of the boat and gave Jesus or the ghost (either way, it was a stupid idea) a dare: "Oh, yeah? If you're really Jesus, tell me to come out there on the water to you!" (Peter, Peter, Peter...what *were* you thinking, buddy?) Je-sus said, "Come on!"

And the next thing you know, Pete hopped over the edge of the boat and stood on top of the water! We don't really know how many steps he took, but we always picture him taking three or four before thinking to himself, *This should not be possible*! And in that moment of unbelief, Peter started to sink. He yelled out to Jesus, who was instantly there, popping Petey back to the surface of the water and back into the boat.

Now—here's why Petey's our hero: Sure, he doubted a little and started to sink. But he's the *only* disciple who got to experience walking on water! There were 11 other disciples in that boat: 11 other guys who saw Jesus walking on the water; 11 other disciples who heard Peter's "dare" to Jesus or a ghost; 11 other disciples who heard Jesus tell Pete to come walk on the water. But those 11 all sat there in the boat.

If you want to really experience life, you have to take some risky steps of faith! You have to get out of the boat.

HOW MUCH DOES GOD LOVE ME? (HOSEA AND GOMER)

One of the greatest and trippiest stories in the Bible is in the Old Testament book of Hosea (say ho-ZAY-uh). God wanted to paint a picture for his people, the Hebrew people (and eventually, for us). So—get ready, here it comes—he told Hosea to marry a prostitute!

God was a creating a living metaphor of his love for us. (Have you learned about metaphors in school—when you use one thing to describe another thing?) In this story, Hosea represents God; the prostitute...well, that's us. That's because we're all so hot-and-cold in our commitments to God. Right after camp, we're totally pumped about God. But a few months later, we don't give God a passing thought unless we're in the car on the way to church.

But here's the wild, surprising truth. God didn't have Hosea marry a prostitute so God could show us what unfaithful maggots we are. It's *so* much better than that!

Hosea married Gomer. (Really, that was her name. But remember, *you're* Gomer! Ha! Okay, back to the story...) For a while Gomer was faithful to Hosea. But then she left him and went back to her prostituting ways, had a couple more kids (by different men), and started living with some other guy. Hosea assumed the marriage was over.

But then God came to Hosea and said (you can see this in Hosea 3:1-3):

"Go, show your love to your wife again, though she is loved by another and is an adulteress. Love her as the LORD loves the Israelites, though they turn to other gods and love the sacred raisin cakes." So I bought her for fifteen shekels of silver and about a homer and a lethek of barley. Then I told her, "You are to live with me many days; you must not be a prostitute or be intimate with any man, and I will live with you."

Sacred raisin cakes? A homer of barley? Don't sweat it—here's the summary: Hosea found his wife and bought her (like, he had to pay the pimp she worked for) so she could come back and be his wife again.

Does this story sound familiar to anyone? When we totally stray from God and love other things more than him, God buys us back with Jesus' death and resurrection to show us how much he loves us. See, God's love for you isn't connected to you being "good" or "bad" or anything in between. God loves you just because God loves you.

GOD LOVES LOSERS (MIGHTY MEN IN 1 AND 2 SAMUEL)

In 2 Samuel 23:8-23, you can find the absolutely amazing superhero-like stories of a group of guys referred to as "David's Mighty Men." (They even sound like a group of superheroes, don't they?). The stuff these guys did, with God's help, is mind-blowing!

Like Abishai (say AB-bish-shy), who went to battle against 300 guys all by himself (and won!). And, get this...all Abishai had was a spear—not the most lethal weapon against 300 guys.

Or how about Shammah (say shuh-MAH)? This mighty man went to battle with a bunch of other guys, but his fighting buddies all chickened out and ran away. Not Shammah, though—he stood in the middle of a field of beans ("This is God's turf, and I'm going to defend it!") and beat down the enemy army all by himself!

There's a *fantastic* story of three of the mighty men overhearing King David being homesick and talking about how much he would love a sip of water from the well by his home. So these three guys slipped through enemy lines, went all the way through enemy territory, and snuck up to the well (which was guarded by the enemy), just to bring David a sip of the water he was homesick for!

But you know what we love about these guys more than anything else? We love that they are remembered as "mighty men" and that God used them in such amazing and powerful ways...but they didn't start that way. Really, they were a bunch of losers.

Back in 1 Samuel 22:1-2, we read about King David being on the run from a guy named Saul who wanted to kill him. And David hid out in a cave. The Bible says, "All those who were in distress or in debt or discontented gathered around him, and he became their leader." See? A bunch of losers! Those were the guys who became (say it with us), "the mighty men"!

Here's the survival tip: We're all losers! We two—Kurt and Marko—we *know* we are. And we're not trying to be mean, but you are, too. All of us are imperfect; *everyone* has things about them that make them losers. But so what?! We all become massive winners through Jesus Christ. Just like the "mighty men," we're used-to-be losers, so we become something new and wonderful with God!

ELEAZAR AND STANDING ALONE

The previous bit was about David's mighty men (you might want to read it before you read this one). But there's one guy in particular we want to point out to you. His name was Eleazar (el-ee-AY-zar).

In 2 Samuel 23:9-10, we read a tiny little summary of a huge, epic story. All of David's fighting dudes—there were at least 400 of them—went out to a spot where their enemies the Philistines were gathered. And David's men taunted them. That means they talked smack!

But the Philistines didn't appreciate the smack-talk so much and decided to fight. What did most of David's dudes do at this point? They ran! But not Eleazar. The Bible says he "stood his ground and struck down the Philistines till his hand grew tired and froze to the sword." It also says, "The LORD brought about a great victory that day."

A great victory—but Eleazar (with God's help) was the only guy fighting! It's so cool that his hand grew tired and froze to his sword, because we need to do the same thing! (No, we don't mean that you should grab a real sword and start slashing!) The Bible calls itself a sword a bunch of times. That's because the message of the Bible can cut right into us, deeply, just like a sword into flesh.

So here's a great survival tip, straight from the life of ol' Eleazar: If you're really going to choose to live for God, you won't always have people to stand with you—sometimes you have to stand alone (of course, God is standing with you!). And the *only* way to survive those stand-alone times is to let your hand freeze to the sword. In other words, it's super important for you to connect, at a really deep level, with the Word of God...the Bible. That's what will give you the strength to stand alone when the time comes! Be like Eleazar, and let your hand freeze to the sword!

AARON AND HUR AND THE IMPORTANCE OF CHRISTIAN FRIENDS

In Exodus 17:8-13, there's a very cool story about getting tired. No, really. Moses had just led the Hebrew people out of slavery in Egypt, and now other armies were attacking them. I mean, come on—give the people a break!

Moses had this cool staff (not a group of people who worked for him, but a stick, like a big walking stick). He had a bit of history with it that we won't go into here, but let's just say that it was a super-stick-of-power (God's power, that is). So during this one battle, Mo stood at the top of a hill overlooking the battlefield. And he held the stick (which he called "the staff of God") in the air. And the Hebrew people started winning.

Now *you* try to hold a big ol' stick in the air for a long time. You can't do it! Your arms start to burn and get weak, and eventually you drop your arms. Well, bummer that it is, that's what happened to Mo. And when he dropped his arms (and his staff), the Hebrew peeps started losing the battle. Raising his arms = winning the battle. Letting them down for a rest = losing the battle. It must have been pretty annoying.

But then—ready for the cool part?—Mo's buds came to his rescue. Aaron (actually his brother, but clearly one of his best friends, also), and another guy named Hur (would you be ticked at your mom if she named you that?) held up Moses' arms for him. And the Hebrew army won the battle.

Here's the survival tip: In the last bit (about Eleazar), we talked about standing alone. But *most* of the time, if you're going to survive your teenage years with your faith in one piece, you're going to need friends who can help you. You're going to need friends who can support you in your desire to live for God, to make good choices, and to stay away from bad choices.

Do you have that kind of friends? Do you have friends who will hold up your arms?

SECTION 9

WHAT'S GOD WANT OUTTA ME?

WHAT DOES GOD WANT OUTTA ME?

Wow, this is such a huge question. And if you ask 100 people, you'll get 100 different answers. And *most* of those answers would probably be true—or at least partially true.

But we're going to sum things up with two little statements. What's God want from you? Two things: everything...and whatever you can give him.

Okay, that doesn't make sense at all, does it? Sorry, let us explain.

What's clear all through the Bible—from beginning to end—in story after story and command after command is that God wants all of you. God wants your complete devotion. (Do you know that word? It means being 100 percent committed to something or someone.) God wants your focus and worship and attention and heart and obedience. God wants to be involved in your plans and dreams and hopes. And God wants every thought, every decision, and every question to come to him.

See? Everything. God wants everything. And it seems fair enough, since he invented us! Even *more* than that, he knows us perfectly (since he invented us)...way, way better than we know ourselves. So giving him everything is really the best thing for us.

So, okay—God wants everything. But we also said God wants whatever we can give him. Check this out: God's reason for inventing us, and God's reason for wanting everything from us, is that he completely loves us. This is a bit upside down from what we would expect. We would think God wants everything from us because he wants to control us. We only think that because that's how *we* would be if we were God! But that's not how God is. God's reason is love.

And because God's reason is love, God won't zap you with zits if you only give him 20 percent instead of 100. You're the one who'll miss out, because giving God 100 percent is the best thing *for you*. But God loves us so much, he's willing to take any attention and worship and love and devotion we give him. And he'll accept it. He won't say, "I don't want *anything* from you if you don't give me *everything*!" That's amazing.

Here's the survival tip: Give God everything. It's the best way to live your life! But when you realize you've only been giving God 20 percent, don't beat yourself up. Just start over again. God is cool with re-starts!

WHY DOES GOD CARE IF I GROW?

You probably don't remember it, but you used to be a one-year-old. And you were cute, too! You waddled around your house in a diaper with a bottle in one hand and your blankie in the other. By the time you were three, a sippy cup replaced your bottle, and instead of a blankie you carried around your favorite copy of *Curious George*.

This may feel a little weird, but go with it: Picture yourself right now...at your age...walking around the house in a diaper. You get a little thirsty so your mom brings you soda in a sippy cup. When it's time for bed, you ask one of your parents to read you a *Curious George* story. It's interesting how something that was perfectly natural at one point in your life now seems totally ridiculous! A one-year-old in a diaper is cute; a middle schooler in a diaper is just plain disturbing. The reason is a simple one: You have grown up *physically*, and as you've grown, you've developed new skills, interests, and abilities.

Just like we grow physically, God wants us to grow *spiritually*. He hopes we will grow in our understanding of him and in our ability to live lives that show our love for him. He hopes that as we get older, our interest in him will increase. Check out this verse:

> *For this reason, since the day we heard about you, we have not stopped praying for you and asking God to fill you with the knowledge of his will through all spiritual wisdom*

and understanding. And we pray this in order that you may live a life worthy of the Lord and may please him in every way: bearing fruit in every good work, growing in the knowledge of God. (Colossians 1:9-10)

Hopefully your life is a lot more exciting now than it was when you were a year old. The main reason is that you've grown up. God hopes our relationship with him continues to get more and more exciting. That's why he wants us to grow!

THE BIG LIST O' RULES (REALLY JUST TWO)

If people are being totally honest (which most aren't), most think of Christianity as a big list of rules. Really, most people think of *all* religions that way. Two huge lists of rules, actually: one list of all the things you have to do, and one list of all the things you can't do.

But you know what? That's not what Jesus said! There *are* a ton of rules in the Old Testament (called "the law"), most of which have nothing to do with us today but were written to protect the Hebrew people and separate them from the people around them.

One time Jesus was teaching (you can read this story in Matthew 22:34-40), and a group of religious leaders who didn't like him started asking him questions to trick him, or at least to show that he didn't really know that much (which, of course, didn't work). One of the groups, the Pharisees, had one of their smartest dudes ask Jesus a tricky question: What's the greatest commandment? (This was a tricky question because the Jewish people believed that all the commandments and rules from the Old Testament were equally important.)

Jesus basically said, "Love the Lord your God with all your heart, with all your mind, and with all your soul." Then he quickly followed that with: "And the second greatest commandment is like it—love your neighbor as yourself. Everything else in the Bible fits under these two."

Wow—that clears things up! There are really only two biggie rules. If we want to really live for God, we don't have to remember a *huge* list o' "things I gotta do" and another *huge* list o' "things I can't do." We just have to remember, and live out, two rules: Love God and love others. Everything else fits under the umbrella of those two!

DOES GOD REALLY HAVE A PLAN FOR MY LIFE?

Most middle schoolers aren't big planners. Sure, you may plan what you're going to do with your friends on Saturday or what outfit you're going to buy with your allowance, but you probably leave the big plans to the grown-ups.

We've got some news for you: Most adults aren't any better at planning than you are! They just fake it so it looks as though they have their acts together. Most people, young and old, just take life as it comes. They go through life with an attitude that says, "Whatever happens, happens." Since most people don't have any plans for their lives, it kinda freaks them out to think that God might! Is it really possible that God has a plan for each of us, that he has a picture in his mind of how our lives should play out?

In the book of Jeremiah, the Bible tells us that God has good things planned for each of us. He doesn't say exactly what those good things are, but you can trust him!

See, God does have a plan for your life, but he probably won't wake you up in the middle of the night and shout it in your ear. It's not that he couldn't do that, but that's not how he usually operates. And don't ask us—we don't know what God's plans are for your life (we don't even know what God's plans for our *own* lives are!).

Are you wondering about things like what college to attend, whom you're going to date, what you should do for a career someday, and all the other important stuff? Does God actually care about all that stuff and

plan it out? Sure! But in God's eyes that stuff's not the most important stuff. God's important plans for us are that we (like we note in the previous chapter) love him with all we've got and love others as much as we love ourselves. When we follow those plans, all the other important stuff in life will work out just fine.

HOW TO LIVE FOR JESUS WITHOUT LOOKING LIKE A JERK

Have you ever met a Christian who was a jerk? When I (Kurt) was in high school, a guy bought an old ice cream truck and changed it into a "Jesus-mobile." Every day at lunch, he would drive up and down the street in it yelling stuff out of the speaker on top of the truck (the same speaker that used to play the ice cream song...). He'd yell stuff like, "You are all going to hell!" and "God hates sinners!" He'd always be sure to toss in a "Jesus loves you!" to wrap up the lunch hour.

My friends laughed at the guy, threw things at the Jesus-mobile, and talked about how stupid Christians were. I was a Christian, too, but I didn't want people to think I was like the Jesus-mobile guy. Your story may be different, but you can probably remember a time when somebody who claimed to be a Christian did some really stupid stuff that made you embarrassed to admit you were one, too.

Is it possible to be a Christian without acting like a jerk? We think so. Especially if you avoid these top three habits of a "Christian Jerk":

1. Christian jerks believe they're better than everybody else. They love to point out all the bad stuff about everybody else while ignoring the bad stuff in their own lives.

2. Christian jerks try to force their beliefs on others. They love to argue and attempt to make others agree with them and think like they do.

3. Christian jerks focus on the outside, not the inside. They forget that God is more concerned about people's hearts than about the clothes they wear, the color of their hair, or how "Christian" they act.

The best way to live for Christ without looking like a jerk isn't just to live *for* Jesus, but to try to live *like* Jesus! Jesus talked to people about God, he challenged them to live better lives, and he spoke up when things weren't the way they were supposed to be. But Jesus was *never* a jerk! He was gentle, humble, caring, and forgiving. Jesus didn't have a "Jesus-mobile" with a loudspeaker. He just walked through life looking for ways to show people how much God loved them. Your friends have probably seen plenty of Christian jerks. Maybe all they really need to see is a Christian who will walk through life like Jesus did.

MY PART IN GOD'S FAMILY

When you became a Christian, you became part of God's family. In fact, the Bible says God adopts you as his child.

Families can be crazy, though. Every family is different, and each of us plays a special part in our families. The family of God is no different: It's very special, and all of us play a part in it. That sounds good, but just what is it about God's family that's so special and different?

It's really big! God's family is made up of every Christian on the planet. God has millions and millions of kids.

It's really diverse! By diverse we mean that there's a lot of variety in God's family. God's kids are rich and poor. God's kids are short and tall. God's kids are male and female. God's kids are young and old. God's kids are all different looking and come from all different races. God's kids are all of that stuff and a whole lot more. Every one of God's kids, including you, is a handcrafted masterpiece who's different from anybody else in the family!

It really needs you! God's family needs you in order to be complete. Without you God's family would miss a really important member! Once you're in God's family, you're in it for good. There have probably been times when you didn't feel like you belonged in his family. Maybe sometimes you don't feel like you're good enough to be called one of God's kids. The family of God isn't made up of people who are "good enough"! It's important to remember that everybody in God's family is a super-important and valuable part of it. Church is one of the places God's family gets together to encourage each other, and your church needs you.

Take a second to think about your own family. You aren't exactly like everybody else in your family. If you have brothers or sisters, you may be almost exactly opposite from them! These differences don't hurt the family; they're what help make the family stronger and more complete.

Your part in God's family is simply to be yourself. You bring stuff to his family that nobody else does, and he needs you to help make his family stronger and more complete. God has wired you a certain way and hopes you will use your abilities, your personality, and your experiences in life to make a difference in the world and to invite others to join his family.

Lots of people say, "My faith is a personal, private thing." Sorry, we don't want to be mean to those people, but that's just lame. It's stupid, really. Sure, there's a sense that only you can decide what you're going to believe—so it's a personal thing that way. But we who know Jesus Christ have stumbled onto the very best way to live! Saying that's a private thing is pretty much like saying to any of your friends who don't know Jesus, "I want you to have a miserable life."

But lots of people—especially teenagers—get all freaked out at the idea of sharing anything about Jesus with their friends. They think they have to know everything and be able to explain everything and answer every question. And they're afraid it will make them look like dorks.

The cool thing is, that's not what we see in the Bible. What we see in the Bible is that people just told their personal stories and the part Jesus played in them.

Two quick examples: In John 9, Jesus healed a guy who was blind from the time he was born. And when people bugged the guy with all kinds of questions about how this healing was possible or what power Jesus had to heal him, he just answered over and over, "All I know is, I was blind, and now I can see. Jesus healed me!"

And in John 4, Jesus talked to a Samaritan woman (she's often called "the woman at the well"). After their conversation, she ran back to her village to tell everyone her story: "Come, see a man who told me everything I ever did"

See, no one expects you to have all the answers. But everyone can tell his or her story!

What's your story? What difference has Jesus made in your life? *That's* the story you should tell to your friends!

GIVING MY TIME

It seems as though people are busier today than ever—especially middle school students. When we were in middle school, there really wasn't much else happening. We'd come home from school and sit around, hoping to find something fun to pass the time. But life for you gets really busy really easily. You play sports all year round, you're in a couple of after-school clubs, you have tons of homework, and you probably go to church once or twice a week. When you do find yourself with a little free time, you probably spend it hanging out online, playing video games, or reading really cool books about middle school life! None of that stuff is bad. Heck, both of us enjoy going online, playing video games, and reading books, too!

But when you look around, it's pretty easy to see that lots of people are using some of their free time to do stuff that helps others and makes the world a little bit better. When a disaster like a hurricane or tsunami happens, people from all over the world chip in to help out. In the inner city, caring volunteers tutor and mentor children. Volunteers who enjoy sports and spending time with kids coach the sports teams you play on.

You're probably good at lots of stuff. In fact, take two minutes and make a mental list of everything you're good at. It'll probably take more time than that, but two minutes should give you a good start. God gave you those gifts and abilities for a reason: *So you can use them!* Not so you can use them just for your own fun and excitement, but so you can make a difference!

Are you good at sports? Then maybe you can help coach a team of younger kids.

Are you good at math? How about asking your math teacher if he knows of anybody who needs extra help?

Do you like little children? The children's department at your church is probably looking for extra help!

Life keeps us really busy. But most of our time is taken up being busy doing stuff that only helps ourselves. What if you slowed down just enough to spend some of your time doing something that makes a difference in someone else's life?

GIVING MY TALENTS

If you're reading this book in order, you'll probably notice that this chapter is a lot like the last one. In fact, this chapter is almost like part 2 of the last chapter. So you may want to read the chapter on giving your time before you read this one.

Jesus told a story about a landowner who was going away on a long trip. Before he left, he pulled aside three of his servants and gave them each some money to take care of while he was gone. He was gone for a really long time, and when he finally came home, he called his servants to see what they had done with his money (in the Bible, this money was called a "talent"). Two of the three servants had used the money in creative ways to make even more money for the landowner. He was super excited and thankful. The third servant didn't do so well, though. He played it safe and did nothing with the money. Instead of using it to make more money for the master, he just dug a hole in the ground and hid it. In his way of thinking, it was better to play it safe than to take a chance and risk losing the landowner's money.

That doesn't sound terrible, does it? Well, it must have been, because the master was totally ticked off! He called the servant evil and lazy because he didn't try to use the money he had been given. The story doesn't say this, but it seems as though the landowner just wanted the three servants to do something...anything...with the money he left them. It would have been better for the third servant to take a risk and lose the money than to just bury it and not use it at all.

God has given you lots of gifts. You are good at lots of stuff. If you're a Christian, you are God's servant, and God gave you these talents to make a difference in our world. He doesn't care if you try and fail. He understands that using your talents for him feels a little risky. He's okay with all that. In fact, part of growing in your Christian faith is practicing using the gifts, talents, and abilities God has given you. When you start using your talents, you'll find out pretty quickly that things won't always work out exactly the way you think they should. The truth is you'll probably make lots of mistakes. But that's okay, because the biggest mistake is playing it safe, taking no risks, and doing nothing with what God has given you.

GIVING MY MONEY AND MY STUFF

Money. We can't do much without it, it's pretty tough to get, and it seems as though we always need more! Almost everything in life requires money. The clothes in your closet, the food on your table, your skateboard, your scrapbook, the home you live in...all this stuff was acquired with money. That's why most of us always want more of it.

Here's the deal: There's absolutely nothing wrong with money, and there's nothing wrong with having lots of it. The Bible has a ton to say about money, and Jesus taught about money a whole lot. When you read the Bible, you'll find out what God thinks about money and how he wants us to think about it, too. We could probably write an entire book about money, but we won't. Instead we just want to help you think a little bit about your money and the stuff your money buys:

It's not yours! Seriously, it's not. The Bible reminds us that everything belongs to God; he's the supplier of all our stuff. In a way, God is loaning you the money and the stuff you call "yours."

You can't take it with you! Someday, hopefully someday a long time from now, you are going to die. When you go to heaven, you won't be taking your money with you. Money and the stuff your money buys is only good while you're alive.

God wants you to be generous! Because your money and your stuff is really just a gift from God, he hopes you'll be generous instead of greedy and stingy. One of the main reasons God has given you so much is so you can turn around and look for ways to generously give back.

> "ONE TIME, WHEN I WAS, LIKE, FIVE YEARS OLD,
> I PUT A QUARTER IN THE OFFERING PLATE AT CHURCH."
>
> —JEREMY, SEVENTH GRADE

Generous people are happier people! When you think it's all yours and you deserve more, you're probably going to hold on to your money and your stuff a lot more tightly. The tighter you hold on to it, the more greedy and selfish you become. We've noticed that some of the happiest people around are the people who have figured this out. It seems as though the more people give, the happier and more meaningful their lives become.

NOBODY SAID IT WOULD BE EASY

Jesus spent a lot of his time talking to people and inviting them to become his followers. You'd think Jesus would have tried to get people on his side by promising an easier way of life or by promising to make all their problems disappear. Because he was God, he could have done that, but he didn't. Instead Jesus spent a bunch of his time making sure people understood what they were getting themselves into. He wanted to make sure people knew that following him wasn't going to be easy.

Here are a few examples:

In Matthew 19:16-22, a young guy who was super rich asked Jesus what it took to become one of his followers. Jesus told him that in order to follow him, he would have to sell everything he had and give it to the poor. Ouch! There's nothing easy about that, is there? In fact, the guy decided it wasn't worth it, so the Bible says he walked away.

Another time a guy told Jesus that he was willing to follow him anywhere. When Jesus heard that, he reminded the guy that foxes have holes to live in and birds have nests, but Jesus didn't have a place to sleep at night. Jesus was always on the go, and the people who decided to follow him had to be willing to give up the comforts of home.

There's even a verse in the Bible that says some people will hate us because we love Jesus. Yikes! Nobody wants to be hated, but that's one of the things that happens when you decide to follow Jesus.

If somebody tells you being a Christian is easy, they're clueless! The Bible promises that living for Jesus is the best way to live, and that Jesus gives us the gift of heaven, but it also makes it pretty clear that deciding to live for Jesus...to follow him...isn't an easy choice. Jesus wants us to think differently, speak differently, act differently, and look at life differently from the way people who don't follow him do. There's nothing easy about that!

The easy choice would be to play by your own rules and do whatever you want to do—but you didn't make the easy choice. And we're proud of you for that!

SECTION 10

SOME OF THE BIGGIES YOU'LL FACE

PEER PRESSURE

In the last chapter we talked about how following Jesus isn't an easy choice. One of the tough things about being a Christian is peer pressure. In fact, when teenagers are asked what the toughest part about being a Christian is, the number-one answer is almost always peer pressure. Let us explain how it works...

Your friends want you to do something you don't want to do—it could be anything. You feel a little bit of pressure because you don't want to miss the fun—and you don't want to be teased or look like a goody-goody, either. The result: Peer pressure.

Another example: Your friend is struggling in math and came up with a perfect way to cheat on the upcoming test without getting caught—cheating from your test! Since you always get As on your tests, you're the perfect candidate. The result: Peer pressure.

Ready for the bad news? Peer pressure will never go away. It just looks different as you grow older.

But here's the good news: You can learn to handle it! Here are a few tips to help:

Know what you believe before you get into a situation. A lot of the pressure you feel is because you're trying to figure out how to handle a situation as it's happening. But if you decide ahead of time that cheating is wrong, it's easier to handle the pressure when it comes. If you decide ahead of time not to see R-rated movies until you're older, the pressure won't seem as tough when your friends ask if you want to head to one next Friday night.

It's okay to get teased. Sure, your friends may tease you or get upset if you decide not to give in to the pressure, but that's okay! A little teasing is probably better than doing something you know you shouldn't.

Being strong earns respect. They may not show it at the time, but when you don't give in to peer pressure, your friends (if they're really your friends) will begin to respect you a little bit more. In fact, you'll be surprised to know that some of them feel the same way you do but have been too scared to do what's right.

Ask God for strength. The best thing to do when facing peer pressure is to ask God to give you the strength to do the right thing. He'll be happy to help!

TEMPTATION

Temptation—sometimes you see it coming, and sometimes you don't. Let's go back to the beginning for a second. Remember Adam and Eve? They're probably most famous for being the first people to mess up big time. Eve was just hanging out when she came face-to-face with a snake (actually the devil in disguise). Now, you'd think Eve would take off running after seeing the snake, but this snake had something to say...literally. It told Eve that if she ate from the tree that God had said was off-limits, she would become as smart as God. The snake said God was trying to hold back some good stuff from Adam and Eve, and that's why he didn't want them to eat from the tree. You see, before the first sin ever happened, Eve experienced the world's first temptation! (And Adam doesn't get off the hook—the Bible says he was *right there* with Eve during the conversation with the serpent and didn't fight the temptation, either.)

Lots of people think that being tempted is wrong, that Christians shouldn't be tempted. That's just not true! Adam and Eve couldn't have done anything to avoid being tempted that day in the garden. They were just going about their business, and there it was...temptation! Still not convinced? How about this one: Jesus was tempted. Yep, it's true. The devil showed up while Jesus was in the desert and tried to get him to do a bunch of stuff he knew he shouldn't do. Jesus never sinned, but he sure was tempted.

Back to Adam and Eve. Their mistake wasn't the fact that they were tempted—their mistake was giving in to the temptation and doing something they knew they shouldn't.

"IT SEEMS LIKE I GET TEMPTED 100 TIMES A DAY. WHY DOESN'T GOD JUST MAKE TEMPTATION GO AWAY?"

—BECCA, EIGHTH GRADE

Wouldn't it be great if becoming a Christian meant that you would never be tempted again? But since that doesn't happen, what should you do? There's no magic formula, but here are three things to remember about temptation:

1. Temptation happens to everybody! It isn't a sin to be tempted.

2. You don't have to give in to temptation. God will help you handle every temptation that comes your way.

3. Temptation is a chance to grow closer to God. Every time you choose not to give in, your faith grows a little bit stronger, too.

MAKING WISE CHOICES

You make thousands of choices every day. Most of the choices you face are about basic stuff: What to wear, where to eat, whether or not to brush your teeth, how to do your hair, and so on. They're all pretty simple choices that don't make a huge difference in your life (although your dentist would disagree about the importance of brushing). But there are some choices that really do make a difference. When you face the biggies, you'll want to make sure you make wise choices.

A few years back, I (Kurt) made the choice to buy a car I didn't even want. I was at a car lot "just looking" when a salesman showed me a car on sale...a sale that was ending that day. I agreed to talk about it, and a few hours later, I was driving home in a car I didn't want or need. I was the victim of peer pressure—pushy-used-car-salesman pressure! I like to blame the pushy salesman, but the truth is, I made the choice to buy the car, it was a bad choice—and it was a big choice.

Here are a few ideas that may help you make wise decisions when you're faced with a big choice:

Slow down! Don't make a big decision too quickly. People make most of their bad choices because they don't take time to really think about them.

Talk to people you trust. When faced with a big choice, it's always a good idea to talk it over with your parents, your youth pastor, or a friend you trust and respect. You'll be surprised how willing people will be to help you work through the decision you're facing.

Think it through. What's the worst thing that can happen? What's the best thing that can happen? How will this choice affect me? How will this choice affect my friends or my family? Ask these kinds of questions and think through the choice.

Pray about it. The Bible says that God gives us wisdom when we ask him for it. Ask God to help you make the right choice.

MY FAITH

I WAS A MIDDLE SCHOOL DORK!
—MARKO

When I was in middle school, my dad's office was in the middle of some woods. But parts of the woods were being cleared for new houses. One Sunday after church, my dad had to stop by his office, and my friend and I wanted to go running through the woods. But my parents were worried I'd get my nice clothes dirty. (Get this, here's what I was wearing: white jeans, white belt, and white dress shoes, all nicely complemented by a maroon button-up shirt. Hey—gimme a break—I was lookin' *hot* for 1977!)

Anyhow, my parents said we could walk in the woods if we *promised* not to get dirty at all. Bad choice: We promised.

A few minutes later we were poking around one of the home construction sites. There was a huge pond—about the size of four houses—that was filled with muddy sludge from the melting snow (it was winter in Michigan). But in the middle of the pond was a *huge* ice-island, about 20 feet across. I thought it would be *so cool* to get out there and stand on that ice-island, like a penguin floating on a piece of ice in Antarctica!

So my friend and I found a giant door, and sure enough, it floated. Somehow we managed to get over to the ice-island, one at a time. I felt like a victorious explorer, ready to stake my country's flag in this newfound land! But while I was jumping up and down with excitement, the whole massive piece of ice made a big, bad sound.

And it moved.

Then it started to sink.

Slowly—really slowly.

It was like a horror movie scene: My friend and I were in complete panic, running around and screaming, trying to get off the island, while the ice was sinking very, very slowly. My friend got on the floating door and made it back to "the mainland." But then he gave the door a lousy push, and it stopped halfway between him and me—out of reach for both of us.

I stood in the middle of Marko Island, my own little ice-land, and slowly watched the muddy water cover my white shoes, then my white pants, passing my white belt, and soaking my maroon shirt. It was then that I decided to swim.

My parents weren't happy. And when I tried to blame it on the "sinking ice-island of death," I didn't make things any better.

RANDOM SURVIVAL TIPS

GOD SINGS ABOUT YOU!

It's fun to have a favorite Bible verse. If you pick one, it's okay to let it change from time to time. My (Marko's) favorite for a long time now is a little verse you've probably never heard in your life, in a Bible book you'd have a hard time finding. It's Zephaniah 3:17. We'll save you the time and print the verse here:

> *The LORD your God is with you,*
> *he is mighty to save.*
> *He will take great delight in you,*
> *he will quiet you with his love,*
> *he will rejoice over you with singing.*

Wow. Seriously, you gotta read that, like, 20 more times! I mean, just look at the first two lines! It wouldn't be all that helpful to have a mighty and powerful God if he was never *with* us! And who wants a God who's always around, but isn't mighty? Then he'd be no different from your little brother!

But our God—*the* God—is both. He's *with* you every day, every second, ready to show his love to you. And he's super powerful, too!

Then check out those last three lines. God takes great *delight* in us and in you. Wow. There are so many days when we feel so unlovable. You're going to feel that, too, if you haven't already. But God doesn't just tolerate you or "put up" with you. God takes delight in you. God giggles with joy when he looks at you, because he's so proud of you, and so interested in you, and so—well—in love with you!

And there sure are lots of days we need peace. Isn't it amazing to know that God wants to help you quiet down and give you peace? *Ahhhhhhhhhhhh.*

Finally, the most amazing line of all: We don't know if this is "for real" or meant in a more poetic way, but we just love the thought of God loving us so much that he makes up songs about us. (Can you picture God singing a song about you to a few of the angels?) *That's* how much God digs you!

WHAT'S AN HEIR?

No, not a *hair*...an *heir*—it's pronounced "air."

Okay, read these verses first. They're from Romans 8:16-17:

> *The Spirit himself testifies with our spirit that we are God's children. Now if we are children, then we are heirs—heirs of God and co-heirs with Christ.*

So here's the deal. You probably know that, if you've become a follower of Jesus Christ, you've also become "a child of God." God considers us his own children—in the best way that could be meant.

But here's the wild part: God considers us his sons and daughters, so that means we also get to be his heirs. Oh, wait, there's that word (*heir*), and we didn't explain it yet. Sorry.

An heir is someone who gets an inheritance. (See the word *heir*, with a letter moved, in the middle of the word *inheritance*?) So, like, if you had a really rich uncle—and he didn't have any kids—maybe he would name you in his will ("I, Rufus T. Loadedpockets, do hereby leave all of my worldly possessions, and especially my millions and millions of dollars, which can be found in a large shoebox in my bedroom closet, to my niece (or nephew), _____ insert your name here _____".)
Then you would be considered Uncle Rufus' heir. You would in*her*it his stuff.

Are you getting it yet—why it's a *really, really, really* (insert 50 million more *reallys* here) big deal that we're God's heirs? And why that makes us co-heirs with Jesus? Whoa. We need to sit down for a minute...feeling dizzy...might...pass...out...

We're back. It's us, Kurt and Marko—your co-heirs. We get to, with you, inherit all God's good stuff! Woo hoo!

HOW TO FIGURE OUT HOW YOU'RE WIRED

You're special! You're one of a kind! There's no one else quite like you! You're unique! Have you ever thought about that? The fact that when God made you, he wired you a certain way—and the way he wired you is totally different from anybody else. Middle school is a great time to start figuring out how God has wired you—because knowing how you're wired is a big step in figuring out what to do with your life and how to make a difference in the world. So, how do you figure out how God has wired you?

First, it's important to understand that you'll probably never figure it out completely. As life happens, you will grow, change, and constantly discover new stuff about yourself. Here are a few things to think about along the way:

What's my personality? Am I shy or outgoing? Do I like being around lots of people, or would I rather be alone? Am I a risk taker, or would I rather play it safe? Your personality is a big part of how God wired you.

What do I enjoy? What stuff interests me? What hobbies do I enjoy? What stuff do I like to learn about?

What am I good at? What are some of my abilities? What do I seem naturally good at? What have I learned to be good at? You may be good at some stuff you don't even enjoy! For example, you may not enjoy math, but you may be good at it.

What has happened to me? Take a look at your life. What experiences—good and bad—have affected you? God uses the stuff that happens in our lives to help wire us.

Experiment, experiment, experiment! One of the best ways to figure out how you're wired is to try new stuff and put yourself in new situations. The best way to see if you're good at drama is to join a drama class. The best way to see if you enjoy sports is to join a team. You've got your whole life ahead of you, and that means you have plenty of time to figure this stuff out!

You are God's handcrafted, custom-made masterpiece. That feels pretty good, doesn't it?

WISDOM RULES

WISDOM RULE #1—BE LIKE AN ANT!

There's a *huge* difference between "smart" and "wise." Smart means knowing lots of stuff. The ultimate smart would be like a computer—able to hold on to *tons* of information and knowledge. Wise, on the other hand, has more to do with understanding things and having the ability to make good choices. A person can be smart, but not wise. Or a person can be wise, but not all that smart. Or pretty much any other combination!

While it's nice to be smart, wisdom is the thing we should really want to grow in. And God totally wants to see you grow in wisdom.

That's one of the reasons we love this funky little Bible passage from Proverbs 30:24-28 that talks about wisdom by looking at some cute (and some, well, not-so-cute) little creatures. Four little creatures that couldn't hurt you if they tried. Four little creatures that you could squish. But they're wise! And we can learn from them.

The first is the ant. The verse says, "Ants are creatures of little strength, yet they store up their food in the summer." You could try this experiment (doing it in your imagination rather than in real life might make Mom happier!): Drop a cookie in an area where ants might show up. Wait. Sooner or later a few ants show up. After a while, you'll see a superhighway of ants coming and going from the cookie. And if you look really closely, you'll see the wisdom of the ants. They're not like us—they're not just having a massive "eat the cookie" party, filling up their little ant tummies. Instead they're each grabbing an itty-bitty piece of cookie and taking it back to their ant kingdom. Can you see them rebuilding the cookie somewhere underground? And then one day when there's no food, the queen ant will announce, "Today, my fellow patient and wise ants, is the day of...THE COOKIE!" And all the little ants will roar their little ant cheers of joy, then eat.

Here's the wisdom of the ants: They make decisions with the future in mind. What do you want your future to be like? Do you want to be living for God when you're 25, or 45, or 75? Do you want to live the life God has for you, full of cool experiences and meaning? Then you'd be wise (like an ant!) to make decisions *now* that will point you to that *then*. Be like an ant!

WISDOM RULE #2—BE LIKE A CONEY!

The first rule talked about the wisdom of ants. Now we get to the only creature in this list of four (in Proverbs 30:24-28) that you probably haven't heard of. Picture a guinea pig, or better yet, a prairie dog (look one up on the Internet if you still have no clue). Small, furry, cute. Couldn't hurt anything tougher than a leaf. That's the coney.

So why in the world would the Bible want us to think of the coney as *wise*? What if I'm not small, furry, and cute? (Uh, yeah...) Let us tell you a bit about coneys, and then we'll unpack the reason they're considered wise.

Coneys can't defend themselves. They don't have big sharp teeth or dangerous claws. They can't let out a big stinky cloud of nastiness. And where the coneys live (especially back when the Bible was written), tons of animals thought coneys were like a Taco Bell drive-thru: quick and tasty enough.

Coneys live their entire lives close to their homes, which they make in the spaces between rocks—as in a pile of rocks (the Bible verse calls the spaces "crags"). Coneys know they'll become snack food for larger animals if they stray too far from the safety of the rocks where they live. So when one of them looks for food, another coney stands guard. If the guard-coney sees a hawk in the sky, it lets out a certain kind of little squeaky sound, communicating, "Dude! You're about to be talon-licking-good!" And if the guard-coney sees a mountain lion, it lets out a different kind of little squeaky sound, communicating, "Dude! One bite! He can finish you off in *one bite*!"

Now stay with us: Did you know the Bible constantly refers to God as "the rock"? Seriously! The coneys know their safety is in the rock (the verse says so). Here's the wisdom of the coney: Our safety is in the rock—in God. If we stray too far from God, thinking, *Hey, I'm pretty smart—I can do life all on my own!* we're headed for doom. But we show great wisdom when we stay really, really close to our rock, God.

Be like a coney! Stay super close to God.

WISDOM RULE #3—BE LIKE A LOCUST!

It's locust time!

Okay, let's back up a bit. Think about the grasshopper. I'm sure you've held a grasshopper in your hand at some point in your life. And it's no big deal, right? I mean, the wiggling might weird you out a bit, but it's not like you were afraid that, at any second, the grasshopper would reveal giant teeth and bite a huge chunk from your wrist.

But something pretty wild happens when a bunch of locusts get together and decide to go on a road trip (grasshoppers and locusts are basically the same—it's just that locusts do this occasional destructive road-trip process when there's no food left in an area). They become destroyers! A swarm of locusts is almost unstoppable.

A big swarm of locusts can completely mow down a field of corn. A big swarm of locusts has even been known to devour a cow, leaving nothing but the bones! One grasshopper jumps onto the side of a cow? Nothin'! But a giant swarm of locust-power? Burger time!

So there's wisdom in this? Yes, because the Bible, remember, is saying that these four little creatures in Proverbs 30:24-28 are wise! Well, here's the wisdom of the locusts: They know the importance of community. One little grasshopper can hardly do anything. But a big ol' group of locusts are a fierce army!

The next 10 years of your life will be filled with big challenges to your faith. And while it's important to know how to stand alone, there's *huge* wisdom in having Christian friends who will support you in your goal of having a strong faith, of living for God. A wise middle schooler tries to build strong friendships with other Jesus-followers who will help him or her.

Be like a locust! Build Jesus-focused community!

WISDOM RULE #4—BE LIKE A LIZARD!

When I (Marko) was in college, my roommates and I kept two pet iguanas. One was big and nasty looking, but hardly ever moved. His name was Fluffy. The other one was small and sleek and was a total spaz. His name was Butch.

One time, my roommates and I wanted to see if we could get Fluffy to move, so we put him on the floor in the middle of the living room and all backed up. Fluffy shocked us by taking off for the open front door. One of my roommates grabbed him by the tail, and (as lizard tails are designed to do) it popped off in his hand, totally freaking him out as it continued to wiggle. We caught Fluffy, and his tail grew back. Lizards are amazing!

When the Bible was written, the king's palace was the most-guarded place in any kingdom. No one got into the palace unless invited. But those crazy lizards! They were constantly climbing and crawling and sneaking in. Like the Bible verse says (in Proverbs 30:28), they could be caught and tossed out. But they would come back. They were relentless!

Here's the wisdom of the lizard: Be bold and persistent! Being persistent means you never stop trying; you never give up. Check out these verses that talk about how God wants us to be bold and persistent:

Jeremiah 29:13—*You will seek me and find me when you seek me with all your heart.*

Romans 2:7—*To those who by persistence in doing good seek glory, honor and immortality, he will give eternal life.*

Galatians 6:9—*Let us not become weary in doing good, for at the proper time we will reap a harvest if we do not give up.*

Hebrews 10:36—*You need to persevere so that when you have done the will of God, you will receive what he has promised.*

Be like a lizard! Never give up trying to do good stuff; never give up working to make your relationship with God stronger. That's wisdom, baby!

EVERYTHING IS CHANGING—INCLUDING THE WAY YOUR FAMILY INTERACTS. THIS BOOK WILL GIVE YOU SECRETS AND TIPS TO HELP MAKE YOUR FAMILY EVEN BETTER AND SURVIVE THE CHANGES THAT COME ALONG WITH MIDDLE SCHOOL.

My Family
Middle School Survival Series
Kurt Johnston & Mark Oestreicher

RETAIL $9.99
ISBN 0-310-27430-3

LISTEN TO WHAT JESUS HAS TO SAY TO YOU. IN THIS 60-DAY DEVO YOU'LL RECEIVE DAILY LETTERS FROM JESUS AND SPEND SOME TIME JOURNALING YOUR THOUGHTS BACK TO HIM AS YOU TAKE PART IN THE CONVERSATION.

Conversations with Jesus
Getting in on God's Story
Youth for Christ

RETAIL $10.99
ISBN 0-310-27346-3

Visit www.invertbooks.com or your local bookstore.

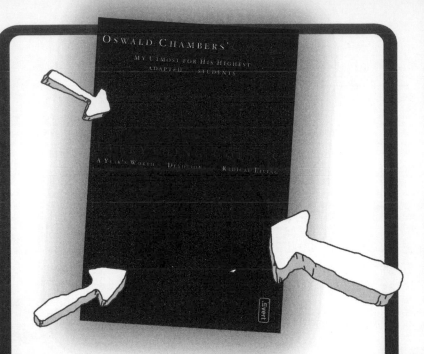